6 Geo. IV.] Newbury and Speenhamland Improvement
Act, with a copious alphabetical index: and a
translation (by W. Illingworth) of the Charter
of Incorporation of the Borough of Newbury.

Anonymous

6 Geo. IV.] Newbury and Speenhamland Improvement Act, with a copious alphabetical index: and a translation (by W. Illingworth) of the Charter of Incorporation of the Borough of Newbury. (An Act for lighting, watching, paving, cleansing and improving the Streets, Highways, and Places, within the Borough Town and Parish of Newbury, and the Tithing or Hamlet of Speenhamland, in the Parish of Speen, in the County of Berks.).

Anonymous
British Library, Historical Print Editions
British Library
1825
xv. 146 p. ; 8°.
010368.w.121.

NEWBURY

AND

SPEENHAMLAND

IMPROVEMENT ACT,

WITH A COPIOUS

ALPHABETICAL INDEX:

AND A

TRANSLATION

OF THE

𝕮𝖍𝖆𝖗𝖙𝖊𝖗 𝖔𝖋 𝕴𝖓𝖈𝖔𝖗𝖕𝖔𝖗𝖆𝖙𝖎𝖔𝖓

OF THE

BOROUGH OF NEWBURY.

—»»●●●««—

PRINTED AND SOLD BY

M. P. PRICE, MARKETPLACE, NEWBURY.

———

1825.

INDEX.

A 2

A 3

6 GEO. IV.   SESSION 1825.

AN ACT

FOR

LIGHTING, WATCHING, PAVING,

Cleansing, and Improving

THE

STREETS, HIGHWAYS, AND PLACES

WITHIN THE

BOROUGH TOWN AND PARISH

OF

NEWBURY,

AND THE

𝕿𝖎𝖙𝖍𝖎𝖓𝖌 𝖔𝖗 𝕳𝖆𝖒𝖑𝖊𝖙 𝖔𝖋 𝕾𝖕𝖊𝖊𝖓𝖍𝖆𝖒𝖑𝖆𝖓𝖉,

IN THE PARISH OF SPEEN,

IN THE COUNTY OF BERKS.

—»»●◉●««—

ROYAL ASSENT, THE 20th MAY, 1825.

—»»●◉●««—

BAKER, TOWN CLERK,

NEWBURY.

DYSON & JONES,
House of Commons.

PRICE, PRINTER,
Marketplace, Newbury.

AN
A C T.

—∞—

Whereas the Borough and Town of NEW-
BURY, in the County of *Berks*, is populous and a
place of trade, and is also a great Thoroughfare for
Travellers:

And whereas the Tithing or Hamlet of SPEEN-
HAMLAND, in the Parish of *Speen*, in the said County
of *Berks*, which immediately adjoins the said Borough
and Town of *Newbury*, is also populous, and being
situated on the High Road from *London* to *Bath* and
Bristol, is also a great Thoroughfare for Travellers;
and several of the Highways, Markets, Streets,
Lanes, Ways, public Passages, and Places within
the said Borough and Town, and the said Tithing or
Hamlet respectively, are not properly paved, repaired, cleansed, lighted, and watched, and are subject to various Nuisances, Annoyances, Encroachments, and Obstructions; and it would tend to the
Protection and Preservation of the Lives and Property of the Inhabitants of the said Borough and
Town, and the said Tithing or Hamlet, and to all
Persons resorting to and travelling through the same,
if the said Highways, Markets, Streets, Lanes, Ways,
Passages, and Places, were properly paved, repaired,
drained, lighted, and watched, and the Nuisances
and Annoyances, Obstructions and Encroachments
therein, were removed and prevented:

B

And whereas the Building comprising the present Town Hall, a Messuage or Tenement now used as a public Victualling House, and the Borough Gaol, is an ancient Building, and very ruinbus and gone to decay; and the same as well as the Butchers' Market underneath the said Town Hall, are inconveniently situated, and not properly constructed for the purposes of public Business:

And whereas the Mayor, Aldermen and Burgesses of the said Borough and Town of *Newbury*, are Owners and Proprietors of the said Town Hall, public Victualling House, Gaol and Market, and the Ground whereon the same stands:

And whereas the building of a new Town Hall and Butchers' Market, with proper Buildings and Accommodations, and also a new Gaol and House of Correction on the same, or on some other convenient spot or spots of Ground within the said Borough and Town, will be a great convenience to the said Borough and Town, and of great public Utility; BUT as the several Purposes aforesaid cannot be effected without the Aid and Authority of Parliament;

May it therefore please your MAJESTY,

That it may be Enacted; And be it Enacted, by the KING's most Excellent MAJESTY, by and with the advice and consent of the Lords Spiritual and Temporal, and Commons, in this present Parliament assembled, and by the authority of the same,

1. THAT the Mayor, Aldermen, and Burgesses for the time being of the said Borough and Town of *Newbury*, and all and every other person or persons who now is or are or shall or may at any time hereafter

be or become the owner or owners of any messuage or
messuages, dwelling-house or dwelling-houses, warehouse or warehouses, or building or buildings, lands,
tenements or hereditaments within the said Borough
and Town, amounting in the whole to the yearly value
of fifty pounds or upwards, and all and every other
person or persons not being an innkeeper victualler or
alehouse-keeper, innkeepers victuallers or alehouse-
keepers, and being tenant or tenants, occupier or
occupiers of the like property as aforesaid, or of
any of the descriptions thereof, situate within the
said borough and town, amounting in the whole to
the yearly value of thirty pounds or upwards, and
all and every person and persons, except as aforesaid,
residing within the said borough and town, and being
possessed of property, real or personal, to the amount
or value of one thousand pounds over and above the
amount of his debts, shall be and they are hereby
constituted appointed and declared to be Commissioners for putting and carrying the several powers
and purposes of this Act into execution, so far as
the same relate to the said borough and town of
Newbury; and that the Lord of the Manor, for the
time being, of the said tithing or hamlet of *Speenhamland,* and the Vicar of the parish of *Speen*
aforesaid, and *George Botham, William Brown,
Charles Bull, Thomas Crofts,* the younger, *Thomas
Chittle, Abner Clarkson, Robert Coster, John Dale,
James Duck, Gabriel Dando, Thomas Darling,
John Dean, William Elliott, George Goddard,
Richard Garrett, Edmund Estcourt Wilkins Gale,
Benjamin Hawkins, Benjamin Hawkins* the younger,
*Charles Hatton, John Hall, John Holloway, William
Jaques, John Neale, John Padbury, Frederick Page,
Henry Seymour, Charles Steward, William Spar-
rowwell, William Stratton,* and also all and every
other person and persons who now is or are or

shall or may at any time hereafter be or become the owner or owners of any messuage or messuages, dwelling-house or dwelling-houses, warehouse or warehouses, or building or buildings, lands tenements or hereditaments, within the said tithing or hamlet, amounting in the whole to the yearly value of thirty pounds or upwards, and all and every other person or persons, not being an innkeeper victualler or alehouse-keeper, innkeepers victuallers or alehouse-keepers, (except any of the persons before specifically mentioned,) and being tenant or tenants, occupier or occupiers of the like property as aforesaid, or any of the descriptions thereof, situate within the said tithing or hamlet, amounting in the whole to the yearly value of twenty pounds or upwards, and all and every person and persons (except as aforesaid) residing within the said tithing or hamlet, and being possessed of property, real or personal, to the amount or value of five hundred pounds over and above the amount of his debts, shall be and they are hereby constituted appointed and declared to be Commissioners for putting and carrying the several powers and purposes of this Act into execution, so far as the same relates to the said tithing or hamlet of *Speenhamland*.

2. Provided always, and be it further Enacted, That no person, except the Mayor Aldermen and Burgesses of the said borough and town for the time being, and the Lord of the Manor of *Speenhamland*, and the Vicar of *Speen*, for the time being, shall be capable of acting as a Commissioner in the execution of this Act, except in administering the oaths or affirmations hereinafter mentioned, until he shall have taken and subscribed before any two or more of the persons qualified as aforesaid, present at any meeting, to be held by virtue of this Act, (and who

are hereby authorized and required to administer the same to each other) one of the two next following oaths or affirmations, as his case may require; and neither the said Mayor Aldermen or Burgesses for the time being, nor any other person, shall be capable of acting as a Commissioner in the execution of this Act, except for the purposes hereinbefore mentioned, until he shall have taken and subscribed in like manner the third oath or affirmation hereinafter set forth.

First Oath:

" I, *A. B.* do swear [*or*, being one of the people " called Quakers, do solemnly affirm and declare,] " That I am really and *bonâ fide* owner of a messuage " or messuages, dwelling-house or dwelling-houses, " warehouse or warehouses, or other building or " buildings, lands tenements or hereditaments, " situate within the borough and town of *Newbury*, " in the county of *Berks*, [*or*, in the tithing or ham- " let of *Speenhamland*, in the county of *Berks*, *as* " *the case may be*] amounting in the whole to the " yearly value of fifty pounds or upwards, [*or*, of " thirty pounds or upwards, *as the case may be*,] " over and above reprizes.

" So help me GOD."

Second Oath:

" I, *A. B.* do swear, [*or*, being one of the people " called Quakers, do solemnly affirm and declare,] " That I am tenant or occupier of a messuage or " messuages, dwelling-house or dwelling-houses, " warehouse or warehouses, or other building or " buildings, lands tenements or hereditaments, " situate within the borough and town of *Newbury*,

" in the county of *Berks*, [*or*, the tithing or hamlet
" of *Speenhamland*, in the county of *Berks*, *as the*
" *case may be*] amounting in the whole to the annual
" value of thirty pounds or upwards, [*or*, twenty
" pounds or upwards, *as the case may be*,] [*or*, pos-
" sessed of an estate, real or personal, of the amount
" or value of one thousand pounds,] [*or*, five hun-
" dred pounds, *as the case may be*, over and above
" the amount of my debts.]
                              " So help me GOD."

Third Oath:

" I, *A. B.* do swear [*or*, being one of the people
" called Quakers, do solemnly declare and affirm,]
" That I will truly and impartially, according to the
" best of my skill and judgment, execute and perform
" all and every the powers and authorities reposed in
" me by virtue of an Act passed in the sixth year of
" the reign of His Majesty King GEORGE the Fourth,
" [*here insert the title of this Act.*]
                              " So help me GOD."

3. And be it further Enacted, That no person
shall act as a commissioner in the execution of this
Act (except in administering the oaths or affirmations
hereinbefore mentioned, and except at the first meeting to be holden under this Act) on the same day
on which he shall himself having taken and subscribed
such oaths or affirmations, or not have taken and subscribed the oaths aforesaid, or being a Quaker, made
and subscribed the affirmation aforesaid, or during the
time he shall hold or enjoy any office or place of trust
or profit under this Act, or be concerned or interested
in any contract made by virtue or in pursuance of
this Act, or in any matter wherein he shall be in anywise personally or beneficially interested, (except as

a creditor on the rates, assessments, or monies herein
directed to be made levied recovered and received);
and if any person not named in or appointed a Commissioner by this Act, or not being otherwise duly
qualified, and not disqualified, or during the time he
shall keep a victualling-house or other house of public
entertainment, or who shall sell wine, ale, beer, cyder,
spirituous or other strong liquors by retail, shall act in
the execution of this Act, every such person shall for
every such offence forfeit and pay the sum of twenty
pounds, together with full costs of suit, to any person
or persons who shall sue for the same, to be recovered
in any of His Majesty's courts of record at Westminster, by action of debt, bill, plaint, or information,
wherein no essoin, protection, wager of law, or more
than one imparlance, shall be allowed; and every
person so sued or prosecuted shall prove that he is
qualified as aforesaid, or otherwise shall pay the said
penalty, without any other proof or evidence being
given on the part of the plaintiff or prosecutor than
that such person hath acted as a Commissioner in the
execution of this Act: Provided always, that all acts
and proceedings of any person or persons acting as a
Commissioner in the execution of this Act, though not
duly qualified as aforesaid, previous to his or their
being convicted of the said offence, shall notwithstanding such conviction be as good valid and effectual as if such person or persons had been duly
qualified to act as a Commissioner or Commissioners
according to the directions of this Act.

4.   And be it further Enacted, that the said Commissioners for the said borough and town of *Newbury*
shall meet and assemble at the Town Hall in *Newbury*,
and the said Commissioners for the said tithing or
hamlet of *Speenhamland* shall meet at the *George and
Pelican Inn* in *Speenhamland*, upon the third *Tuesday*

next after the passing of this Act, between the hours of ten and twelve of the clock in the forenoon, in order to put this Act into execution, and shall afterwards meet in the same place respectively, or at such other place within the said borough and town, or tithing or hamlet respectively, as the said Commissioners respectively shall from time to time direct and appoint, and between the hours aforesaid, on the first *Tuesday* in every month for the purpose of carrying this Act into execution, without any notice being given to the said Commissioners of such meeting; and at all their several meetings the said Commissioners shall pay and defray their own expenses, except any sum not exceeding ten shillings a day for the use of the room wherein they shall meet for the purposes of this Act.

5. Provided always, and be it further Enacted, That it shall be lawful for the said Commissioners respectively, or any two or more of them, to adjourn for any longer or shorter space of time than the first *Tuesday* in the next month immediately subsequent to the last meeting, or to any other place or places than the said Town Hall and *George and Pelican Inn* aforesaid, but that in every such case notice of such adjournments respectively in writing or printed, signed by the respective clerks to the said Commissioners, or any two of the said Commissioners respectively, shall be given by affixing such notice on the outer door of the respective churches of *Newbury* and *Speen* aforesaid, ten days at least before every such meeting.

6. And be it further Enacted, That if it shall at any time or times be thought necessary that a meeting of the Commissioners for their respective jurisdictions should be holden on an earlier day than the first

Tuesday in the month immediately subsequent to the last meeting, or after any adjournment, on an earlier day than the day to which such meeting shall have been adjourned, then and in every such case any two of the said Commissioners respectively, or the clerk to the said Commissioners respectively, (on an order signed by three or more of the said Commissioners respectively, mentioning the time place and purpose, of such earlier meeting, being given to him, or left at his last or usual place of abode,) shall forthwith give notice of the meeting to be holden on such earlier day, in manner before directed, and of the time place and purpose which shall be mentioned in such notice (such time not being less than three days after such notice); and all proceedings of the said Commissioners respectively at such earlier meeting, shall be as good and valid as they would have been in case such Commissioners had met on the first *Tuesday* in the month immediately subsequent to the last meeting, or in pursuance of any adjournment.

7. And be it further Enacted, That no act of the said Commissioners for their respective jurisdictions, shall be or deemed to be good and valid unless made and done at a meeting to be holden as aforesaid by virtue of this Act, (except as may be herein excepted); and all the powers and authorities by this Act granted to or vested in the said Commissioners respectively, shall from time to time be exercised by the major part of them present at any public meeting, the number present at such meeting not being less than five for the said borough and town of *Newbury,* and not being less than three for the said tithing or hamlet of *Speenhamland,* (except in such cases where by this Act a greater number is required); and all the orders and proceedings of the major part of such Commissioners

respectively, present at such meeting, shall have the same force and effect as if the same were made or done by all the Commissioners respectively for the time being; and at every such meeting one of the said Commissioners, to be appointed by a majority of the Commissioners present, shall be chairman, and shall, besides his own vote, have a casting vote in case of an equality of votes.

8. And be it further Enacted, That a proper book or books shall be provided and kept, in which fair and regular entries shall be made of all acts orders and proceedings relative to the execution of this Act, and the names of the Commissioners for their respective jurisdictions who shall be present at the respective meetings to be holden in pursuance of this Act: and such entries, being signed by the chairman of each respective meeting, shall be deemed originals, and shall be allowed to be read in evidence in all courts whatsoever, in all cases, prosecutions, suits and actions touching or concerning any thing done in pursuance of this Act; and such book and books shall at the meetings of the said Commissioners respectively be open and liable to their inspection, and to the inspection of all persons affected by this Act, without fee or reward.

9. And be it further Enacted, That no order made by the said Commissioners for their respective jurisdictions shall be revoked or altered at any subsequent meeting, unless at some meeting to be held for that express purpose, of which seven days notice of the intention of such meeting shall be given by the respective clerks to the said Commissioners, by fixing the same notice upon the outer door of the respective places of meeting aforesaid; and any new work, or alteration of or addition to any former work,

where the same shall be estimated to cost the sum of one hundred pounds, shall not be adopted, or any order made in respect thereof at any meeting within the respective jurisdictions of the said Commissioners, unless notice shall have been given and entered in the book containing the acts orders and proceedings of the said Commissioners respectively at the last preceding meeting of the said Commissioners.

10.   And be it further Enacted, That at a meeting of the said Commissioners for their respective jurisdictions, which shall be held on the third *Tuesday* in *June* yearly, at the respective places hereinbefore mentioned, or to be appointed as aforesaid, the accounts of all monies received and paid from time to time by virtue or in execution of this Act, by any person or persons whomsoever, shall be produced and stated to the said Commissioners respectively.

11.   And be it further Enacted, That it shall be lawful for such of the said Commissioners as are Justices of the Peace to act as such Justices in the execution of this Act, notwithstanding their being Commissioners, except only in cases where they shall be personally interested.

12.   And be it further Enacted, That the said Commissioners for their respective jurisdictions shall and may from time to time, whenever they shall think necessary, by writing under their hands, appoint and employ a treasurer or treasurers, clerk or clerks, assessor or assessors, collector or collectors, receiver or receivers of the rates assessments and monies herein mentioned, and also a surveyor or surveyors, and such other officer and officers, person and persons, for the execution of this Act, as they the said Commissioners respectively shall

think proper; and the said Commissioners shall
and may from time to time remove them, or any of
them, and in like manner appoint others in the room
of those removed, and out of the monies to be raised
by virtue of this Act pay such salaries wages or allowances to the said officers and other persons as they the
said Commissioners respectively shall think reasonable;
and the said Commissioners respectively shall and they
are hereby required to take such security from every
such treasurer collector and other officers as they the
said Commissioners respectively shall think reasonable; and all such officers so to be appointed shall
under their hands, at such time and times and in such
manner as the said Commissioners respectively shall
direct, deliver to the said Commissioners, or to such
person or persons as they shall appoint, true and perfect accounts in writing of all matters and things
committed to their charge, and of all monies which
shall have been received by such officers and persons
respectively by virtue of this Act, and how much
thereof hath been paid and disbursed, and for what
purposes, together with the vouchers for such payments; and shall pay all such money as shall remain
due from them respectively to the said Commissioners
respectively, or to such person or persons as they shall
appoint; and if any such officer or person shall refuse
or wilfully neglect to make and render any such
accounts, or to produce or deliver up the vouchers
relating to the same, or to make payment as aforesaid,
or shall refuse or neglect to deliver to the said Commissioners respectively, or to such person or persons
as they shall appoint, within ten days after being
thereunto required by the said Commissioners respectively, by notice in writing, to be given to or left at
the last or usual place of abode of such officer or person,
all books papers and writings in his custody or power
relating to the execution of this Act, and to give

information and satisfaction to the said Commissioners respectively respecting the same, then and in every such case, upon complaint made by the said Commissioners respectively or any two or more of them, or by any person or persons whom they shall appoint for that purpose, of any neglect or refusal as aforesaid, to any Justice of the peace for the county, city, town corporate or place, such Justice may and he is hereby authorized and required, by warrant under his hand and seal, to cause the officer or person refusing or neglecting to be brought before him, and upon his appearing, or having been summoned and not appearing, or not being to be found, to hear and determine the matter in a summary way; and if upon the confession of the party, or by the testimony of any credible witness or witnesses upon oath or affirmation (which oath or affirmation such Justice is empowered to administer,) it shall appear to such Justice that any of the money which shall have been collected or raised by virtue of this Act, shall be in the hands of such officer or person, such Justice may and he is hereby authorized and required upon nonpayment thereof, by warrant under his hand and seal, to cause such money to be levied by distress and sale of the goods and chattels of such officer and person; and if no goods or chattels of such officer or person can be found sufficient to answer and satisfy the said money and the charges of distraining and selling the same, or if it shall appear to such Justice that such officer or person shall have refused or wilfully neglected to render or give such account, or to produce the vouchers relating thereto, or that any books papers or writing relative to the execution of this Act shall be in the custody or power of such officer or person, and he shall have refused or wilfully neglected to deliver up or give satisfaction respecting the same as aforesaid, then and in any of the cases aforesaid such

C

Justices shall commit such offender to the common Gaol or house of Correction for the county town or place wherein the offence shall be committed, there to remain without bail or mainprize until he shall have made and given a true and perfect account and payment as aforesaid, or until he shall compound with the Commissioners respectively for such money, and shall have paid such composition in such manner as they shall appoint, (which composition the said Commissioners respectively are hereby empowered to make and receive,) and until he shall have delivered up such books papers and writings as aforesaid, or have given satisfaction in respect thereof to the said Commissioners respectively; provided, that no person who shall be committed by virtue of this Act on account of his not having sufficient goods or chattels, shall be detained in prison for any longer term than twelve calendar months; provided also, that if any money shall remain due from such officer or person, officers or persons, the commitment of him or them to prison shall not be deemed a discharge for the same, nor exonerate his or their surety or sureties, but such officer or person, officers or persons, and his or their surety or sureties, shall remain liable to the payment thereof in the same manner as if such officer or person had not been committed to prison.

13. Provided always, and be it further Enacted, That it shall not be lawful for the said Commissioners for their respective jurisdictions to appoint the person who may be appointed their clerk in the execution of this Act, or the partner of any such clerk, or the clerk or other person in the service or employ of any such clerk, or of his partner, the Treasurer for the purposes of this Act; or to appoint any person who may be appointed treasurer, or the partner

of any such treasurer, or the clerk or other person in the service or employ of any such treasurer, or of his partner, the clerk to the said Commissioners respectively; and if any person shall accept both ·the offices of clerk and treasurer for the purposes of this Act, or if any person being the partner of any such clerk, or the clerk or other person in the service or employ of any such clerk, or of his partner, shall accept the office of treasurer, or being the partner of any such treasurer, or the clerk or other person in the service or employ of any such treasurer, or the clerk or other person in the service or employ of the partner of such treasurer, shall accept the office of clerk in the execution of this Act, or if any treasurer shall hold any place of profit or trust under the said Commissioners, other than that of treasurer, every such person so offending shall for every such offence forfeit and pay the sum of one hundred pounds to any person or persons who shall sue for the same, to be recovered with full costs of suit in any of His Majesty's courts of record at Westminster, by action of debt or on the case, or by bill suit or information, wherein no essoign protection or wager of law, nor more than one imparlance, shall be allowed.

14. And be it further Enacted, That if any clerk, treasurer, surveyor, or collector, or other officer employed by the said Commissioners for their respective jurisdictions, for the purposes of this Act, shall exact, demand, take or except any fee emolument or reward whatsoever (other than such salary or allowance as shall be appointed and allowed by the said Commissioners respectively) for and on account of any thing done by virtue of this Act, or for forbearing to do any thing ordered or directed by the said Commissioners respectively, or on any other account whatsoever relative to his employment

or duty, or shall be concerned or interested in any bargain or contract made by the said Commissioners respectively for the purposes of this Act, every such person so offending shall be incapable of afterwards serving or being employed under the said Commissioners respectively, and shall forfeit and pay the sum of twenty pounds for every such offence to any person or persons who shall sue for the same, together with full costs of suit, by action of debt, bill, plaint or information, in any of His Majesty's courts of record at Westminster, within six calendar months after the offence committed, in which suit or prosecution no essoign protection or wager of law, nor more than one imparlance, shall be allowed.

15. And be it further Enacted, That the said Commissioners respectfully, shall and they are hereby required from time to time to order and direct a book or books to be provided and kept by their clerk for the time being, in which book or books such clerk shall enter or cause to be entered true and regular accounts of all sums of money received, paid, laid out and expended, for or on account of the purposes of this Act, and of the several articles, matters and things for which such sums of money shall have been disbursed and paid, and such book or books shall at all seasonable times be open for the inspection of the said Commissioners, and every creditor of the rates hereby authorized to be made, and of every person paying any rate or assessment hereby authorized, or otherwise affected thereby, without fee or reward; and the said Commissioners, creditors, and other persons aforesaid, or any of them, shall or may take copies of or extracts from the said book or books, or any part or parts thereof, without paying any thing for the same; and in case the said clerk shall refuse to permit, or shall not permit, the said

Commissioners, creditors, or persons aforesaid, to
inspect the same, and to take copies or extracts as
aforesaid, such clerk shall forfeit and pay any sum
of money not exceeding five pounds for each default,
to be levied recovered and applied in manner hereinafter provided.

16. And be it further Enacted, That the said
Commissioners for their respective jurisdictions shall
and they are hereby empowered from time to time,
when and as often as they shall think it expedient,
to appoint such number of able-bodied men as they
shall judge proper to be employed as watchmen and
as patrolmen within the said borough and town, and
tithing or hamlet respectively, for the security
thereof, and for preserving good order therein, under
such regulations and subject to such orders as the
said Commissioners respectively shall make and give
from time to time in that behalf; and to provide
watchhouses watchboxes or places for the reception
of such watchmen and patrolmen, and for the safe
custody of such persons as may be apprehended by
such watchmen or patrolmen while on duty, and to
pay such watchmen and patrolmen while on duty
reasonable wages or allowances, and such watchmen
and patrolmen from time to time to remove and dis-
place, and also to appoint one or more fit person or
persons in the stead of any watchman or watchmen,
patrolman or patrolmen who shall die, or who shall
be discharged from his or their office by the said
Commissioners respectively, and also to impose from
time to time any fine not exceeding forty shillings on
any watchman or watchmen, patrolman or patrolmen
for every neglect or misbehaviour (such fine to be deducted out of the wages of such watchman or watchmen,
patrolman or patrolmen, if the amount of such wages
so due are sufficient to answer or pay such fine, and

if such wages so due are not sufficient to pay such fine, the deficiency to be levied in the same manner as any penalty or fine is by this Act directed to be recovered,) and from time to time to make such orders and regulations as they the said Commissioners respectively shall deem expedient, for the better government of the watchmen or patrolmen to be so appointed, and to repeal such orders and regulations or any of them, and to substitute others.

17. And be it further Enacted, That it shall and may be lawful to and for such watchmen or patrolmen, or any of them, and they are hereby empowered and required to apprehend and secure in some proper place or places of security, to be for that purpose appointed within the said borough and town and tithing or hamlet respectively, all felons, malefactors, rogues, vagabonds, beggars, idle and disorderly persons, disturbers of the public peace, nightwalkers, prostitutes, and all suspected persons who shall be found wandering or misbehaving themselves within the said borough and town and tithing or hamlet respectively, and to conduct all such persons as soon as conveniently may be before some Justice of the peace for the county town or place wherein such offence shall be committed, to be examined and dealt with according to law.

18. And be it further Enacted, That in case any watchman or patrolman, to be appointed by virtue of this Act, shall be guilty of any neglect or misconduct in the execution of his duty, it shall be lawful for any Justice or Justices of the peace, within his or their respective jurisdictions, upon complaint against any such watchman or patrolman of any such neglect or misconduct, to commit any such watchman or patrolman to his Majesty's gaol for the county town or

place for any time not exceeding three calendar
months.

19. And be it further Enacted, That if any
victualler or keeper of any inn or public house, or
other person, shall knowingly harbour or entertain, or
suffer to remain in his or her inn or public house, or
any building or outhouse attached thereto, or occupied
therewith, any such watchman or watchmen, patrolman or patrolmen as aforesaid, during any part of the
time appointed for his or their being on duty, every
such victualler or keeper, or other person shall, on
conviction, forfeit and pay any sum not exceeding
five pounds.

20. And be it further Enacted, That it shall be
lawful for the said Commissioners for their respective
jurisdictions to give such rewards in money to the
watchmen and patrolmen respectively to be appointed
as aforesaid, who may be disabled or wounded in the
execution of their office, as they the said Commissioners respectively shall think reasonable, such
money to be paid out of the monies to be raised by
virtue of this Act.

21. And be it further Enacted, That if any person
shall obstruct or assault any watchman or patrolman,
to be employed or appointed by virtue hereof, in the
execution of his duty, every person so offending, upon
being thereof convicted before one or more Justices
of the peace for the county town or place, shall be
liable to a penalty, at the discretion of the said
Justice or Justices, not exceeding ten pounds, or such
Justice or Justices may commit any such person to
the Gaol for the county town or place for any time
not exceeding three calendar months.

22. And be it further Enacted, That all watchmen

patrolmen and sergeants of the night shall be sworn
in as constables before any Justice or Justices of the
peace for the county town or place, and act as such
while in the execution of the powers and authorities
of this Act, and they are hereby invested with and
shall have and enjoy the like powers and authorities,
privileges and immunities, as any constable or constables is or are invested with, or have or enjoy by
law.

23. AND whereas it is expedient for the safety
of His Majesty's liege Subjects that the King's Peace
be constantly kept within the said borough and town,
and tithing or hamlet respectively; BE it therefore
further Enacted, That the Justices of the Peace
acting for the county town or place within his or
their respective jurisdictions, shall, as they shall see
occasion, at any quarter or petty sessions to be holden
in and for the said county town or place, upon application being made to them by the said Commissioners respectively, or any three or more of them,
assembled at any meeting for that purpose, from time
to time appoint a competent number of able-bodied
men as assistant constables of the said borough and
town, and tithing or hamlet respectively, for keeping
the peace therein; and also for executing all such
warrants precepts and orders as the said Justices, or
any of them, shall from time to time direct to the
said constables or assistant constables, or any of them,
to be by them executed within the said borough and
town, and tithing or hamlet respectively, together
with a superior or superintendant of such assistant
constables, such superintendant constable to receive
such allowance or salary as the said Commissioners
respectively assembled as aforesaid shall from time
to time direct; all which superintendant and assistant constables, when appointed, shall be sworn

in as constables before any Justice of the peace of the said county town or place respectively, and shall when on duty be invested with the like privileges powers and authorities, and shall be subject to the like duties, and entitled to the like protection and indemnity, and be subject to the like punishment, penalties and forfeitures, as constables are or shall be from time to time by the laws and statutes of this Realm.

24. And be it further Enacted, that the said Justices, when such constables have been appointed as aforesaid, at their said quarter or petty sessions, shall from time to time order and direct what remuneration shall be made to such constable or constables respectively, for his or their services in the execution of his or their said duties; and also to order and direct any such remuneration to be paid to such constable or constables out of the monies raised or to be raised for the purpose of lighting and watching the markets, streets, squares, ways, lanes and public passages and places, within the said borough and town, and tithing or hamlet respectively, by virtue of this Act.

25. And be it further Enacted, That it shall be lawful for such superintendant and assistant constables, and they are hereby required to patrol the streets, highways, lanes, passages, and other public places within the said borough and town, and tithing or hamlet respectively, on every *Sunday* during such hours as the said Commissioners respectively shall appoint, and to apprehend and secure in such place or places of security as shall be appointed by such Commissioners respectively, all vagrants, rogues, malefactors, and other disorderly persons, who shall be found loitering or misbehaving themselves, or

committing any disorders or offences in the said borough and town, and tithing or hamlet respectively, and to conduct all such persons, as soon as conveniently may be, before some Justice of the peace for the said county town or place respectively.

26. And be it further Enacted, That the said Commissioners for their respective jurisdictions shall, and they are hereby authorized, empowered, and required, when and as often as they respectively shall think it necessary to make one or more separate rate or rates, assessment or assessments in every year, to be signed by the said Commissioners respectively, or any three or more of them, upon the tenants or occupiers of all houses, mills, factories, shops, werehouses, coach-houses, stables, cellars, vaults, or buildings, yards and gardens attached thereto and occupied respectively, and also upon the tenants or occupiers of yards or pieces of ground used for the purpose of trade or business in the said borough and town, and tithing or hamlet respectively, (save and except the market-house, gaoler's house, guildhall, prisons, sessions house, or the poor or workhouse for the use of the poor of the borough of *Newbury* aforesaid, or any houses, buildings, or other hereditaments, used and occupied for the purposes of any public charity,) for the purposes of defraying the charges and expenses of lighting and watching the same, and carrying this Act into execution in respect of the same; and also to make one or more other rate or rates, assessment or assessments, in every year, to be signed by the said Commissioners respectively, or any three or more of them, upon the tenants or occupiers of all lands, tenements, tithes, houses, factories, shops, warehouses, coach-houses, yards, gardens, stables, cellars, vaults, buildings and heredi-

taments, in the said borough and town of *Newbury*, and tithing or hamlet of *Speenhamland* respectively, (except as before is excepted, for the purpose of defraying the charges and expenses of paving, widening, amending, repairing, cleansing, watering, improving, extending, and regulating the said markets, streets, squares, ways, lanes, footways, public passages, and places, and otherwise carrying this Act into execution in respect thereof; and the money or monies so rated or assessed on the said tenants or occupiers shall be paid by them respectively to the collector or collectors, or other person or persons appointed by the said Commissioners respectively to collect the same; and the said rates and the monies arising therefrom shall be and are hereby vested in the said Commissioners respectively.

27. Provided always, and be it further Enacted, That all lands within the said borough, and parish and tithing or hamlet respectively, which, at the time of making any rate or assessment for the purpose of defraying the charges and expenses of paving, widening, amending, repairing, cleansing, watering, improving, extending, and regulating the said markets, streets, squares, ways, lanes, footways, public passages and places as aforesaid, shall be used as arable meadow or pasture ground only, and all orchards, nurseries, gardens or other grounds occupied by gardeners seeking a livelihood by the occupation or cultivation thereof, and all barns, yards, stables, or other buildings principally appropriated to the purposes of husbandry, and all tithes shall be charged and rated at one-half only of the full rate or assessment for the time being directed to be made on houses, mills, factories, shops, and other buildings as aforesaid.

28. And be it further Enacted, That if any tenant

or occupier of any of the premises aforesaid shall neglect or refuse to pay his or her proportion or proportions of any of the said rates or assessments respectively, to the said collector or collectors, or other person or persons, for the space of seven days after demand made thereof, the same shall be levied and recovered on all and every such tenant or tenants, occupier or occupiers so neglecting or refusing, by distress and sale of his or their goods and chattels, by warrant under the hand or seal or hands and seals of any one or more Justice or Justices of the peace, acting for the county town or place within his or their respective jurisdictions, such defaulter having been first duly summoned by such Justice or Justices respectively to appear before him or them at a time and place mentioned in such summons to show cause for such neglect or refusal; and the overplus (if any) of the monies to be raised by such distress and sale shall be returned on demand to the owner or owners of the goods and chattels so distrained and sold, together with what shall remain unsold, after deducting all costs charges and expenses previous to and attending such distress and sale, such costs charges and expenses to be ascertained and directed by the said Justice or Justices; and in default of such distress, it shall be lawful for any such Justice or Justices respectively to commit such person to the gaol for the county town or place wherein the offence shall be committed, there to remain without bail or mainprize for any time not exceeding three calendar months, unless payment shall be sooner made of such sum or sums of money as shall have been found to be due and in arrear upon all or any such assessment or assessments as aforesaid, together with all costs charges and expenses attending the recovery thereof, such costs charges and expenses to be ascertained and directed by the said Justice or Justices.

29.   Provided always, and be it further Enacted,
That it shall not be lawful for the said Commissioners
for their respective jurisdictions to make any rate or
rates, assessment or assessments, for the purpose of defraying the charges and expenses of lighting and watching the markets, streets, squares, ways, lanes, public
passages and places within the said borough and town
of *Newbury,* and tithing or hamlet of *Speenhamland*
respectively, exceeding the sum of two shillings in
the pound in any one year, nor to make any rate or
rates, assessment or assessments, for the purpose of
defraying the charges and expenses of paving, widening, amending, repairing, cleansing, watering, improving, extending, and regulating the said markets,
streets, squares, ways, lanes, footways, public passages
and places; and otherwise carrying this Act into
execution in respect thereof, exceeding the sum of
two shillings and sixpence in the pound in any one
year.

30.   And be it further Enacted, That if the said
Commissioners for their respective jurisdictions shall
at any time or times neglect or omit to rate or assess
any person or persons liable to pay or be charged with
any rate or assessment to be made by virtue of this
Act, or shall in any such rate or assessment overrate
or underrate any person or persons liable to pay any
such rate or assessment, then and in every such case
it shall be lawful for the said Commissioners respectively to rate and assess in the said rate or assessment
such person or persons so omitted to be rated and
assessed, and to lesson or raise the rate or rates,
assessment or assessments of such person or
persons so overrated or underrated, or otherwise
to alter or amend such rate or rates, assessment
or assessments, so as to make the same conform-
able to the true intent and meaning of this Act; and

D

it shall be lawful for the said Commissioners respectively, and they are hereby empowered, to strike out the name or names of any person or persons not liable to the payment of the rates hereby directed to be made, and all such additions to or alterations or amendments in such rates or assessments shall be as valid and effectual as if the same had been part of the rates or assessments originally made, and shall not be held to vitiate the original rate or rates.

31.   And be it further Enacted, That no rate or assessment whatsoever shall be made in pursuance of this Act upon any person or persons for or in respect only of his or their being the occupier or occupiers of any dwelling-house under the annual value of five pounds.

32.   Provided always and be it further Enacted, That nothing in this Act contained shall extend or be construed to extend to authorize or empower the said Commissioners to rate or assess, for the purposes of this Act, any lands tenements or hereditaments which by law are at present exempt from or not changeable with, or subject or liable to, the payment of parochial or other taxes or assessments.

33.   And be it further Enacted, That in all cases where any person or persons shall remove from or quit the possession of any house, building, land, ground, tithes, or other hereditaments, the tenant or occupier whereof shall be rated or assessed, or be liable to be rated or assessed by virtue of this Act, every such person or persons so removing from or or quitting possession of the same shall be liable to pay such rate or assessment in proportion to the time that such person or persons occupied or possessed the same respectively, and in like manner as if such

person or persons had not removed from or quitted the possession of the same ; and in all cases when any person or persons shall come into or occupy any house, building, land, ground, tithes or other hereditaments, rated or assessed, or liable to be rated or assessed as aforesaid, out of or from which any other person or persons shall have removed, or which at the time of making any such rate or assessment, was empty and unoccupied, the person or persons coming in or occupying the same shall be liable to pay such rate or assessment, although his her or their name or names may not be inserted in such rate or assessment, in proportion to the time that such person or persons shall occupy the same respectively, and in like manner as if such person or persons had been originally rated or assessed by name in such rate or rates, assessment or assessments ; which said proportions, in case of dispute, shall be settled and ascertained by the said Commissioners for their respective jurisdictions.

34. And be it further Enacted, That as to and for any messuages or other hereditaments within the said borough and town, and tithing or hamlet respectively, the yearly rent or value of any of which messuages or hereditaments shall not exceed ten pounds, or which shall be let to weekly or monthly tenants, or shall be let furnished, or in lodgings, or in separate apartments, or at rents which shall become payable and to be collected at any shorter period than quarterly, the owner or owners of all and every such messuages or hereditaments shall and may be rated for and in respect of the same accordingly ; and that the person or persons letting such messuages or hereditaments respectively, or claiming or receiving the rents and proceeds thereof, may be from time to time deemed and considered to be the owner and owners thereof, and all and every such owner

and owners from time to time and at all times
hereafter may be rated to the rates to be made by
virtue of this Act, as the occupier or occupiers of
such messuages or hereditaments respectively, unless
the said Commissioners respectively shall from time
to time prefer and determine to rate the actual occupier or occupiers of such messuages or hereditaments
respectively; and the person or persons so rated,
whether the owner or owners, or the occupier or
occupiers, shall from time to time pay, or cause to be
paid, all and every such rates in respect of such
messuages or hereditaments respectively, and upon
nonpayment thereof, such rates may be levied by the
distress and sale of the goods and chattels of such
person or persons respectively, wheresoever they
shall be found, or of the goods and chattels of the
person or persons inhabiting the same messuages or
hereditaments respectively, and may be otherwise
sued for and recovered in like manner in which such
rates may be levied and recovered from any other
persons by virtue of this Act: Provided always, that it
may be lawful for the said Commissioners, if they shall
think proper, to compound with any owner or owners
of any messuages or other hereditaments within the
said borough and town, and tithing or hamlet respectively, the yearly rent or value whereof shall not
exceed ten pounds, or which shall be let to weekly
or monthly tenants, or which shall be let furnished or
in lodgings, or in separate apartments, or at rents
which shall become payable or be collected at any
shorter period than quarterly, for the payments of such
rates for or in respect of such messuages or hereditaments, at such reduced yearly rental as the said
Commissioners respectively shall think reasonable,
not being less than three-fourth parts of the rack rent
or annual value of such messuages or hereditaments
respectively, or to remit to the owner or owners of

any such messuages or hereditaments respectively last mentioned, such part of such rate as the said Commissioners respectively shall think proper, not being more than one third part of the rates to which such owner or owners shall be rated in respect of such last-mentioned messuages or hereditaments respectively, or otherwise to collect from such owner or owners the whole of such rates as they shall think proper; and also that the said Commissioners respectfully may vary discontinue or renew either or any of such compositions as the said Commissioners respectively shall from time to time deem expedient.

35.   AND to prevent disputes touching the designation of owner or landlord or proprietor of any messuages or hereditaments intended to be made liable to be rated by any rates from time to time made by virtue of this Act, or as to any other matters or provisions affecting any owners landlords or proprietors of any messuages or hereditaments in this Act contained; BE it further Enacted, That the person or persons legally authorized and empowered to receive and collect or receiving and collecting, or claiming to be entitled to receive and collect the rents of any messuages or hereditaments from the tenants or actual occupiers thereof, or of any of them, shall be liable to be rated, and shall be compellable to pay the rates in respect of such messuages or hereditaments, in all cases in which either owners or landlords or proprietors are made liable to be rated, and to the payment of the rates made by virtue of this Act; and shall also be liable as such owners or landlords or proprietors, in all other matters, and for all other purposes affecting the owners or landlords or proprietors of any messuages or hereditaments in this Act contained, unless the real owner or owners, or

landlord or landlords, proprietor or proprietors thereof, shall be declared by himself or themselves to be the real owner or owners, landlord or landlords, proprietor or proprietors thereof, or shall be distinctly and certainly known to their satisfaction by the said Commissioners respectively, to be the real owner or owners, landlord or landlords, or proprietor or proprietors thereof.

36.　And be it further Enacted, That the goods and chattels of each and every person and persons renting and occupying any separate part or apartment of or in any messuage or hereditament, and the goods and chattels in every messuage or hereditament let ready furnished, although the person or persons occupying such messuage or hereditament, or separate part or apartment be not rated under or by virtue of this Act, shall be liable to be distrained and sold by virtue of any warrant under the hand and seal of one of His Majesty's Justices of the peace for the county town or place, where he is by this Act authorized and directed to grant for any rates made by virtue of this Act, which have accrued or become due during the term or the occupancy by any such person or persons of any such messuage or hereditament or separate part or apartment thereof, and for the costs charges and expenses of such warrant, and of any appraisement, possession, removal or sale of such goods and chattels, or attendant thereupon; but no such person or persons shall be required or compellable to pay any greater sum for or towards the discharge of the said rates, or of any of them, than the amount of the rent actually due and payable by such person or persons to the owner or owners of such messuage or hereditament, or other person or persons rated as the occupier or occupiers of the messuages or hereditaments so entirely or partly occupied by such person or persons; and that each and every person or persons who shall pay any such rates as ought to have been paid by the owner or owners of any such messuage or hereditament, or by his or their landlord or landlords, or upon whose goods and chattels the same shall be levied in pursuance of this Act, shall and may deduct the same from and out of the rent due and payable, or to become due and payable to his or their landlord or landlords so letting out the same messuage or hereditament or separate part or apartment to him or them (unless there shall be some agreement to the contrary between the landlord and tenant,) and the receipt or receipts for such payment or payments shall be a sufficient discharge for every such person or persons for so much money as he or they shall have so paid, or which shall have been so levied on his and their goods and chattels in pursuance of this Act, and shall be repaid by such owner or owners, or be allowed by such landlord or landlords of such messuages or hereditaments in part or full payment (as the case may be for the rent due or to become due to him or them from such person or persons as aforesaid, for or in respect of such messuages or hereditaments, or separate parts or apartments thereof respectively.

37.   AND for the Purposes aforesaid, and in order to enable the said Commissioners for their respective jurisdictions to light the said borough and town, and tithing or hamlet respectively by gas, and to provide gasometers, cisterns, pillars and other apparatus, and to lay pipes, stopcocks, syphons, plugs, branches and machinery, and for other the purposes of this Act, and to carry this Act into immediate execution in respect thereof; BE it further Enacted, That it shall be lawful for the said Commissioners respectively, or any five or more of them, from time to time to borrow and take up at interest such sum or sums of money, as the

said Commissioners respectively shall judge necessary
for the several purposes of this Act, upon the credit
of the said rates assessments and monies to be made,
levied, collected and received by virtue of this Act,
for lighting paving and watching the said borough and
town, and tithing or hamlet respectively; and by
writing under their respective hands and seals to
assign all or any part of the said last-mentioned rates
assessments or monies to such person or persons as shall
lend or advance any money thereon, or to his, her, or
their trustee or trustees, as a security for the principal
money to be advanced, with interest for the same;
and the charges and expenses of such assignment
thereof (to be made as hereinafter mentioned) shall be
from time to time defrayed by the said Commissioners
respectively out of the monies so borrowed: and every
such assignment shall be in the words or to the effect
following:

    " WE   of the Com-
" missioners acting in execution of an Act of Par-
" liament made in the sixth year of the reign of King
" GEORGE the Fourth, intituled, [*here set forth the*
" *title of this Act,*] In consideration of the sum of
"   advanced and lent by
" upon the credit and for the purposes of the said
" Act, Do hereby grant and assign unto the said
"   his executors, administrators and
" assigns, such proportion of the rates assessments and
" monies to be raised, levied, collected, and received
" by virtue of the said Act, as the said sum of
" doth or shall bear to the whole sum which may at
" any time be borrowed, or become due and owing,
" or be charged upon the credit of the said rates
" assessments or monies; To be had and holden
" from this   day of   until the said sum of
"   with   interest at   per centum per annum

" for the same, shall be repaid and satisfied. In
" witness whereof we the said Commissioners have
" hereunto set our hands and seals, the day of
"   in the year   ."

And all such assignments respectively shall be numbered, commencing with number one, and so proceeding in an arithmetical progression ascending,
whereof the common excess or difference shall always
be one ; and every such security shall be good valid
and effectual, and shall entitle the person or persons
to whom the same shall be made, his, her, or their executors administrators and assigns, to the payment
thereof, and to all profit and advantage thereof, according to the true intent and meaning of this Act.

38. And be it further Enacted, That it shall be
lawful for the persons entitled to any of the securities
for the money to be borrowed upon legal interest as
aforesaid, and their respective executors administrators or assigns, (as the case may be) at any time,
by writing under their hands and seals, to transfer
such securities to any person or persons whomsoever ;
and every such transfer may be in the words or to
the effect following :

" I,   being entitled to the sum of
" .   secured to   and his assigns,
" [or, his executors, administrators, and assigns,] [as
" the case may be,] by virtue of an assignment bear-
" ing date the   day of   under the
" hands and seals of   the Commissioners
" acting in the execution of an Act of Parliament
" made in the Sixth year of the reign of King
" GEORGE the Fourth. intituled, [here set forth the
" title of this Act,] upon the credit of the rates,
" assessments, and monies granted or payable by

" the said Act, Do hereby transfer all my right and
" title in and to the same sum, and all interest and
" other money now due and arising thereon, unto
"   his executors administrators and assigns.
" Dated the   day of   ."

39. And be it further Enacted, That a copy of
every security or assignment, together with the number or numbers thereof, and an extract or memorial
of every transfer thereof respectively, shall be entered in a book to be kept for that purpose by the
clerk to the said Commissioners for their respective
jurisdictions, which extract or memorial shall specify
and contain the date, names of the parties, and sums
of money thereby transferred, to which book any
person interested shall at all seasonable times have
access, and shall have free liberty to inspect the
same without fee or reward; and for entering every
such transfer, the said clerk shall be paid by the
person to whom such transfer shall be made, the sum
of two shillings and sixpence, and no more; and
every such transfer, after entry thereof as aforesaid,
shall entitle the person to whom the transfer shall
be made, and his or her executors, administrators,
and assigns, to the benefit of the security thereby
transferred, without any other registry or enrolment
whatsoever.

40. Provided always, and be it further Enacted,
That in case the said Commissioners for their respective jurisdictions can at any time borrow or take up
any sum or sums of money at a lower rate of interest
than the assignments or securities which shall be
then in force shall bear, it shall and may be lawful
to and for the said Commissioners respectively to
charge the said rates, assessments or monies in manner aforesaid, with such sum or sums of money as

they shall think proper, and the interest thereof at
such lower rate as aforesaid, and to pay off and discharge the assignments or securities bearing a higher
rate of interest, according to the directions and
regulations herein prescribed for paying off assignments or securities.

41. And be it further Enacted, That when any
sum of money shall be borrowed or taken up at interest upon the credit and security of the said rates
or assessments, the sum of ten pounds per centum per
annum on every such sum shall, if the said Commissioners shall think it expedient after the passing of
this Act, or at any time hereafter to adopt a Sinking
Fund, from thenceforth to be charged on this Act,
and be appropriated and paid out of the rates duties
and assessments, over and besides the interest payable
on the money borrowed, in order to form a sinking
fund for the gradual payment of all principal sum and
sums so to be borrowed, and as often as the said sinking
fund shall amount to the sum of two hundred pounds,
then and in such case that sum shall be applied in the
payment of an equal amount of the said principal
money then due and owing on the credit or security
of the said rates or assessments rateable, or by lot
among the creditors, as the said Commissioners shall
think proper.

42. And be it further Enacted, That all the money
to arise by the said several and respective rates, assessments, and other monies hereby granted and allowed to
be assessed and levied or received under or by virtue
of this Act, shall be paid to the treasurer to the said
Commissioners for their respective jurisdictions, or to
such other person or persons as they shall appoint;
and separate accounts shall be kept of all such rates
and assessments and sums of money, under the separate

heads of the several and respective purposes for which
the same have been levied or received, and shall be
applied and disposed of from time to time in defraying
the charges and expenses of lighting, watching,
paving, repairing, cleansing, watering, extending,
and amending the markets, streets, squares, ways,
lanes, and other public passages and places of and in
the said borough and town, and tithing or hamlet respectively, and in paying and defraying all expenses
which the said Commissioners respectively and their
officers shall necessarily sustain or be put unto in
carrying this Act into execution, and in prosecuting
or defending any prosecutions, actions, or suits in
any matter relative to the execution of this Act, or
of any thing to be done under or by virtue thereof,
and for such other uses and purposes as are herein
expressed, all which said monies shall be severally
and separately applied to the several and respective
purposes for which the several and respective rates
and sums shall be levied and raised, and to and for
no other purposes whatsoever.

43. And be it further Enacted, That all the
present and future pavements in the several markets,
streets, squares, ways, lanes, and other public passages and places within the said borough and town,
and tithing or hamlet respectively, and the stones
gravel and other materials of which, as well as the
footways as carriageways of such markets, streets,
squares, ways, lanes, and other public passages and
places, do and shall consist, and all the dirt, dust, dung,
ashes, soil and filth to be swept gathered and collected
in or from those places, or any of them; and also all
lamps, lamp irons, lamp posts, fire engines, and the
pipes buckets and other materials thereunto belonging,
watchboxes, watchhouses, and other houses and
buildings, and all other matters and things which

shall hereafter be used erected or fixed up by virtue
of this Act; and all materials implements and other
things which shall be purchased or provided by the
said Commissioners respectively for the purposes of
this Act, shall belong to, and be the property of, and
are hereby vested in the said Commissioners respectively; and the Commissioners for the borough and
town of *Newbury*, shall be known by the name of
" The Commissioners for the Improvement of the
" Borough and Town of *Newbury*, in the County of
Berks;" and the Commissioners for the tithing or
hamlet of *Speenhamland* shall be known by the name
of " The Commissioners for the Improvement of the
" Tithing or Hamlet of *Speenhamland*, in the County of *Berks*;" and the said Commissioners respectively shall and may cause to be brought any action
or actions, suit or suits, or direct the preferring of
any bill or bills of indictment, as the case may require,
against any person or persons who shall steal, take,
or carry away, detain, spoil, injure, or destroy the
several articles and things hereby vested in them the
said Commissioners respectively as aforesaid, or any
of them, or any part or parts thereof; and in all
such actions, suits and bills of indictment respectively,
it shall be deemed and taken to be sufficient to state
generally that the article or articles, thing or things,
for or on account of which such action or actions,
suit or suits shall be brought, or bill or bills of indictment preferred, is or are the property of " the Com-
" missioners for the Improvement of the Borough
" and Town of *Newbury*, in the County of *Berks*,"
or of " The Commissioners for the Improvement of
" the Tithing or Hamlet of *Speenhamland*, in the
" County of *Berks*," (as the case may be,) without
particularly stating or specifying the name or names
of all or any of the said Commissioners respectively;
and the said Commissioners respectively shall have

E

power and authority from time to time to sell and dispose of, for the purposes of this Act, all or any of the said articles and things, or any part or parts of the same respectively, to such person or persons, and in such a manner as they the said Commissioners respectively shall think proper.

44. And be it further Enacted, That it shall be lawful for the said Commissioners for their respective jurisdictions, and they are hereby authorized, empowered, and required, from time to time to cause the present or any future markets, streets, squares, ways, lanes and other public passages and places, within the said borough and town of *Newbury*, and tithing or hamlet of *Speenhamland*, to be repaired, amended, raised, lowered, widened, extended, or altered, both in the carriage and footways, and to be from time to time amended and kept in good repair, upon such levels and in such manner, and with such sorts and kinds of materials as they shall judge necessary and proper; and also to cause the said markets, streets, squares, ways, lanes and other public passages and places to be cleansed, lighted, watched, and watered, in such a manner as the said Commissioners respectively shall think proper; and all encroachments, obstructions, nuisances, and annoyances therein to be removed, and drains, sewers, sinks, gutters, and watercourses to be made for conveying water off and from the said markets, streets, squares, ways, lanes and other public passages and places, in such manner as they the said Commissioners respectively shall think proper; and that no person shall, without the consent of the said Commissioners repectively, alter the form or break up the ground or pavement of the carriage or footways, within any of the said markets, streets, squares, ways, lanes or other public passages and places, or make the same other-

wise than as directed by the said Commissioners respectively, upon pain of forfeiting any sum not exceeding ten pounds for every offence; and such person so offending shall also pay to the surveyor or other person so appointed by the Commissioners respectively to receive the same, all costs, charges and expenses of restoring the ground of such carriageway or footway to its former state; and all such penalties, costs, charges, and expenses shall be levied and recovered in like manner as any penalty is by this Act directed to be recovered.

45. AND whereas there are several lanes, courts, passages and places within the borough and town of *Newbury,* and the tithing or hamlet of *Speenhamland* aforesaid, which are not public highways, or repaired by virtue of the public Highway Acts; BE it therefore Enacted, That it shall be lawful for the said Commissioners, or any five or more of them, to view and inspect any such lane, court, passage or place within the said borough and town of *Newbury,* and the tithing or hamlet of *Speenhamland,* which now is or hereafter may be built upon, or in building, but not paved; and if upon such view they shall be of opinion that the same, or any part or parts thereof, is or are fit or proper to be paved, the said Commissioners, at any meeting to be held in pursuance of this Act after such view, and after special notice thereof given to each Commissioner, specifying the object of such meeting, and at which not less than seven Commissioners shall be present, shall and may order the surveyor of the highways for the said parish, or any other person, to give notice to the owner or owners, proprietor or proprietors, lessee or lessees of any such land or ground, or of any house, shop, warehouse, coach-house, stable, cellar, vault, tenement or hereditaments in any such lane, court, pas-

sage or place, or may leave such notice at his or her or their last and usual place of abode, or with his, her or their known servant or servants, or if no such owner or owners, proprietor or proprietors, lessee or lessees, can be found, then such notice may be stuck against the premises to which the same shall relate, or any part thereof, which notice shall require such owner or owners, proprietor or proprietors, lessee or lessees, to meet such Commissioners at the time and place therein mentioned (not being less than ten days from the date of such notice) to compound for the paving thereof; and at such meeting so to be held such owner or owners, proprietor or proprietors, lessee or lessees, shall be offered the option either to lay down and complete such pavement upon such footway and carriageway, in such manner and within such time, as the said Commissioners shall in that behalf direct, or otherwise to pay a composition for such paving, at any rate not less than one half of the sum at which the surveyor or inspector of the said pavements for the time being shall estimate the actual costs and expenses of laying down and completing such pavement, whether carriageway or footway, upon condition of the actual payment of the amount of such composition to the collector in that behalf, appointed, within ten days after demand thereof (which composition the said Commissioners are hereby authorized to enter into, and thereupon to cause the footways and carriageways as to which such composition shall be entered into, to be paved in such manner as the said Commissioners shall seem fit); and if any such owner or owners, proprietor or proprietors, lessee or lessees as aforesaid, shall not by himself or themselves, or by his or their agent or agents, attend at the time and place at which he shall be desired to attend for the purpose aforesaid, or shall not agree with the said Commissioners for such composition as aforesaid, or having so agreed shall not pay the amount of such composition within ten days after demand made by the collector authorized to receive the same, then and in any of those cases it shall be lawful for the said Commissioners to order the footways or carriageways to which such notice, or such composition as aforesaid shall relate, to be paved as soon as conveniently may be, and in either of the said cases all the charges and expenses attending such paving shall be paid by such respective owner or owners, proprietor or proprietors, lessee or lessees as aforesaid, and shall be recovered and levied upon the goods and chattels of such owner or owners, proprietor or proprietors, lessee or lessees, in like manner as any rate or rates, assessment or assessments, made by virtue of this Act, is or are herein made recoverable.

46. And be it further Enacted, That the said Commissioners for their respective jurisdictions shall have full power and authority to cause all or any of the highways, streets, squares, ways, lanes and other public passages and places within the said borough and town, and tithing or hamlet respectively, to be watered when where and as often as need or occasion shall be or require, and for such purpose to cause such number of wells and pumps to be dug sunk and made in any of the said highways, streets, squares, lanes or other public passages and places as may be necessary, and from time to time to alter the same as there shall be occasion, provided that no such well or pump shall be sunk or made so as to injure any house or other building, or any vault or cellar under any of the said highways, streets, squares, lanes, or other public passages or places.

47. And be it further Enacted, when any of the

streets ways or lanes within the said borough and town, and tithing or hamlet, which are already laid out, or which shall hereafter be laid out in any part of the said borough and town, and tithing or hamlet respectively, shall be well and sufficiently made and paved, or otherwise put in good order and repair, and completed to the satisfaction of the said Commissioners respectively, or any five or more of them, assembled at any meeting for putting this Act into execution, it shall be lawful for the said Commissioners respectively, so assembled as aforesaid, or any five or more of them, and they are hereby empowered, with the consent of a majority of the owners or proprietors of the several houses, buildings, lands, tenements or hereditaments within such streets ways or lanes, from time to time to declare the same to be public highways, and from and after such declaration made, and not sooner, the same and every of them shall be deemed and taken to be public highways to all intents and purposes; and it shall also be lawful for the said Commissioners respectively to connect any such streets, or open the same into any other streets or public highways, with consent of the owner proprietor and occupier of the lands houses and premises which may intervene and be necessary to use for such purpose: Provided always, that the said Commissioners respectively shall not be empowered to make such declaration of or concerning any front streets which shall be of less width than ten yards in the narrowest part thereof, or of and concerning any back streets which shall be of less width than six yards in the narrowest part thereof, except such streets as were actually laid out and begun to be built upon previous to the passing of this Act.

48. Provided also, and be it further Enacted, That all new streets which shall hereafter be made in

the said borough and town, and tithing or hamlet respectively, and all public streets already laid out but not paved, shall be paved and completed by the person or persons laying out and appropriating the land for such new streets, in such manner and in such proportions as shall be ordered and directed by the said Commissioners respectively, so as that such new streets shall be made and completed with pavement and footways in like manner as the other parts of the said borough and town, and shall hereafter become subject to the like rules and regulations as to the future care and repairs thereof as the other streets of the said borough and town.

49. Provided always, and be it further Enacted, That in case the person or persons laying out and appropriating the land for such new street or streets, shall not pave and complete the said new street or streets in manner aforesaid, within two calendar months after notice given so to do by the clerk to the said Commissioners for their respective jurisdictions, it shall and may be lawful to and for the said Commissioners respectively, by writing under their hands, to order any such street to be paved and completed, and the costs and charges thereof shall be paid and reimbursed to the said Commissioners respectively, or their order, by the person or persons appropriating the land for such new street or streets, and in default of payment thereof on demand, the same may be recovered in like manner as any penalties or forfeitures are by this Act authorised to be recovered.

50. And be it further Enacted, That for the better carrying this Act into execution, it shall and may be lawful to and for the said Commissioners for their respective jurisdictions, and they are hereby empowered from time to time as they shall see occasion,

to describe and determine the limits and extents of the several markets, streets, squares, ways, lanes, public passages and places within the said borough and town, and tithing or hamlet respectively, which shall be within their jurisdiction under the powers of this Act, in such manner as they shall think proper, (subject nevertheless to the power of the Mayor Aldermen and Burgesses, and the Mayor for the time being for the said borough and town, to remove, alter, vary or extend the said markets as hereinafter mentioned ;) and shall and may paint engrave or describe, or cause to be painted engraved or described, on a conspicuous part of some house or other building at or near the corner of every such market, street, square, way, lane, public passage and place, the name or number by which such market, street, square, way, lane, public passage or place now is or shall be called, and may order and direct the several houses, shops, warehouses and buildings within the said several markets, streets, squares, ways, lanes, public passages and places, or any of them, to be numbered with figures painted or placed on the door of every such house, shop, warehouse or other buildings, or such other part thereof, as the said Commissioners respectively shall think proper ; and if any person shall wilfully destroy obliterate or deface any of such names or numbers, or any part thereof, or cause or procure the same to be done, every person so offending shall for every such offence forfeit and pay any sum not exceeding five pounds : Provided always, that nothing herein contained shall extend or be construed to extend to authorize the said Commissioners to interfere with, or in any matter to alter or affect any power or authority given or belonging to the said Mayor Aldermen and Burgesses or to the Mayor for the time being of the said borough and town, by any charter, law, custom or usage, to remove, alter vary and extend, all or any of the public markets and market places of the said borough and town, or to set out any new or other public markets and market places, or to remove, alter, vary and extend such new or other public markets and market places, and to ascertain the limits thereof in case of any dispute or question in relation thereto.

51. And be it further Enacted, That when any such number or numbers, figure or figures, painted or put on any house, shop, warehouse or other building, or on the door or doors thereof, within the said borough and town and tithing or hamlet respectively, shall be defaced or rubbed out, the owner or owners, occupier or occupiers of such house, shop, warehouse or other building, where the number or numbers, figure or figures, shall have been so defaced or rubbed out, shall, upon personal notice given to him her or them, or upon notice in writing left at such house, shop, warehouse or other building, signed by the clerk to the said Commissioners respectively, cause the same number or numbers, figure or figures, to be in the same manner painted or put on such house, shop, warehouse or other building, or on the door thereof respectively, within seven days after such notice, and in case of neglect or refusal to comply with such order, every such owner and occupier shall forfeit and pay for every such offence any sum not exceeding five pounds.

52. And be it further Enacted, That if any person or persons shall upon any of the footways or foot pavements within the said borough and town, and tithing or hamlet respectively, run, draw, drive or carry any truck, wheel, sledge, wheelbarrow, handbarrow, bier or carriage whatsoever, or any wheel or other part of any such carriage, or carry any sedan chair (no person

being therein), or roll any cask or tub, other than for
the necessary loading or unloading thereof, unto, upon,
from or out of any carriage, for any longer space than
the extent of the premises in the occupation of the
person from or to whose house or building such cask or
tub shall be rolled (such premises adjoining to or having
immediate communication with such house or building
from or to which such cask or tub shall be rolled;)
or if any person shall wilfully drive any cart or carriage
whatsoever, or shall ride lead or drive any horse or
other beast or any cattle whatever, on any of the said
footways or foot pavements (except in the necessary
crossing the same in passing to or from any stable or
stables or premises immediately adjoining such footways or foot pavements,) or set any cask, tub, pail,
bucket, stool, bench, stall, or any other matter or thing,
so as in any manner to cause any obstruction or impediment in the footway or on the pavement; or shall in
any market, street, square, way, lane or other public
passage or place, within the said borough and town
and tithing or hamlet respectively, hoop, fire, cleanse,
wash, or scald any cask or tub, or hew saw or cut any
stone wood or timber, or bore any timber, or make or
repair any coach, chaise, waggon, sledge or other
carriage (except such as may want immediate repair
for any sudden accident on the spot, or which cannot
conveniently be removed for that purpose, such un-
avoidable repair to be done and completed with all
convenient speed) or if any person shall hang out or
cause to be hung out any linen, or cloth, or any
article of wearing apparel, or other article for
the purpose of sale, or of airing the same, upon
or from any door or window, or from the front of any
house, shop or premises adjoining or within any
market, street, square, way, lane, public passage or
place within the said borough and town, or fix or tie
up any line, rope or cord for any such purpose, or

shall fix up any flowerpot or bowpot or pots at any window or windows without sufficiently guarding the same, so as to prevent their being blown or thrown down; or if any person shall in or upon any market, street, square, way, lane, public passage or place, within the said borough and town and tithing or hamlet respectively, shoe, bleed, farry or kill any horse or other beast or cattle; or if any person shall within any market, street, square, way, lane, or other public passage or place, within the said borough and town and tithing or hamlet respectively, (except only in such places as the said Commissioners respectively shall direct,) show or expose any stallion or stone-horse, or expose to sale any horse or other beast, or turn or drive loose any horse, mare, mule, or ass, or ride or lead any horse, mare, mule, or ass for the purpose of exercising or airing the same; or if any person shall make or assist in making of any bonfire, or let off or fire any gun, pistol, blunderbuss or other fire-arms (except in self-defence,) or any serpent or rocket, or throw any cracker, squib or other fireworks, or play at football, or any other game or games, to the annoyance of any passenger or passengers, or shall blow any horn or trumpet, or use any other noisy instrument, to the annoyance of any of the inhabitants of the said borough and town, or tithing or hamlet respectively, or for the purpose of hawking, selling or distributing any articles whatsoever, or for the purpose of calling or collecting passengers, parcels or goods; or if any person shall kill or slaughter, or shall scald, singe, dress or cut up any animal, either wholly or in part, in any such markets, streets, squares, lanes, public passages or places, or cause or permit any blood to run from any slaughter-house, butcher's shop or shambles into the same, or any of them; or shall slack water or mix any lime mortar or cement, or shall hang up place or expose to sale any goods, wares or merchandize whatsoever, or any fruit, vegetables or garden-stuff, butchers meat, pastry, confectionery, or other matter or thing, in upon or projecting over any part of the footway or carriageway of any such markets, streets, squares, ways, lanes, public passages or places, so as to obstruct or incommode the passage of any person, carriage or horse therein; or shall cause any privy or necessary house within the said borough and town and tithing or hamlet respectively, to be emptied, except within the hours of twelve of the clock at night, and four of the clock in the morning; or shall at any time throw out of any door or window upon any such carriageway or footway, or into the stream or brook in *Northbrook Street*, in *Newbury* aforesaid, any water or filth, or the contents of any utensil or vessel whatsoever; or shall lay deposit or spill, or shall be caused to be laid deposited or spilt, the contents of any such privy or necessary house, or any part thereof, upon any carriageway or footway within the said borough and town, or tithing or hamlet respectively; or shall for the purpose of obtaining or collecting manure, or for any other purpose, stop up or impede the passage of any common sewer, ditch or watercourse; or if any person shall wilfully obstruct the passage of any person upon any footway or crossing in the said borough and town, or tithing or hamlet respectively; or if any person or persons shall permit or suffer his her or their mastiff, bulldog or any other dangerous animal to go at large without being safely and sufficiently muzzled, or shall permit or suffer any dog whatsoever to go at large within the said borough and town, or tithing or hamlet respectively, after any public notice given for one week by handbills, published within the said borough and town, or tithing or hamlet respectively, by or under the order and direction of the said Commissioners respectively, during such time as such notice shall direct such dogs to be confined on account of any suspicion of canine madness ; or shall cause any bull, bear or other animal to be baited with dogs within the said borough and town, or tithing or hamlet respectively, or shall commit or permit any other kind of obstruction or annoyance in or upon any such street, way, lane, public passage or place within the said borough and town, or tithing or hamlet respectively, then and in every such case every person so offending shall for every such offence forfeit and pay any sum not exceeding five pounds ; provided nevertheless, that nothing herein contained shall extend or be construed to extend so as to prevent or hinder any person or persons from placing by lawful authority any stall, booth, stool, bench or form for the sale of any goods or wares, or from exposing to sale any meat, poultry, vegetables, fruit, or any other matter or thing, in any marketplace or street within the said borough and town, and in such place and on such day or days as are now or shall hereafter be permitted by the said Mayor, Aldermen, and Burgesses, or their successors, or by the mayor for the time being, so as such stall, booth, stool, bench or form be not placed upon any footpath within the said borough and town, and so as there may be free access to the houses, shops and other buildings in the said marketplace or street.

53. And be it further Enacted, That if after the passing of this Act, any waggon, cart, dray or other carriage shall be left to stand or remain in or upon any market, street, square, way, lane, public passage or place within the said borough and town, or tithing or hamlet respectively, with or without horses or other cattle, for any time longer than shall be necessary for the loading or unloading thereof, and in case the same shall not be standing during the time of the

F

loading or unloading thereof as near to the side of such market, street, square, way or lane, passage or place, or if any stage coach, diligence, postchaise or other carriage let to hire, shall be left to stand or remain in any of the said markets, streets, squares, ways, lanes, passages and places as aforesaid, with or without horses, or for any longer time than shall be necessary for the taking up or setting down of the passengers thereof, and for loading or unloading their baggage; or if any sacks of grain, potatoes, fruit, or any timber, bricks, tiles, lime, limestones, slates, hay, straw, woods, faggots, coals, boards, tubs, goods, wares or merchandize, or other materials or things whatsoever, shall be laid or placed, or left to remain in or upon any of the said streets, squares, ways, lanes, public passages or places, either in the carriage way or footway, for any longer time than shall be necessary for moving and housing the same; or if any broken glass or earthenware, ashes, rubbish, dust, dirt, dung, filth, or any other nuisance or annoyance whatsoever, shall be wilfully thrown or cast into, or laid in or upon any of the said markets, streets, squares, ways, lanes, public passages or places, then and in every such case the driver or other person, so leaving every such waggon, cart, dray, coach, diligence, postchaise or other carriage to stand or remain, and the person or persons who shall have so laid placed or left such sacks of grain, potatoes, fruit, or any timber, brick, tiles, lime, limestones, slates, hay, straw, wood, faggots, coals, boards, tubs, goods, wares or merchandize, materials or other things, in or upon any of the said markets, streets, squares, ways, lanes, public passages or places, and the person and persons who shall wilfully throw, cast or lay, or cause to be thrown, cast or laid any broken glass or earthenware, ashes, rubbish, dust, dirt, dung, filth, or any other nuisance or annoyance, into or upon any of the said markets, streets, squares, ways, lanes, public passages or places, shall for every offence in any of the cases aforesaid forfeit and pay any sum not exceeding twenty shillings; provided nevertheless, that no person shall be subject to any penalty by virtue of this Act for or on account of any building materials, rubbish or dirt being in or upon any of the said markets, streets, squares, ways, lanes, public passages or places, before or near the house or building of such person, occasioned by the building or pulling down, rebuilding or repairing such house or building, so as there be convenient room left for carriages to pass, and a sufficient way kept clear for foot-passengers, and so as the owner or occupier of such house or building do cause such materials, rubbish and dirt to be removed out of such market, street, square, way, lane, public passage or place, within a reasonable time after such building, pulling down or repairing shall be finished, or upon notice to be given to him or her, in manner hereinafter directed for the serving of notices, signed by the clerk to the said Commissioners for their respective jurisdictions, and so that during the time the same shall be lying in such market, street, square, way, lane, public passage or place, such owner or occupier shall guard and fence off the same, either by a temporary railing or otherwise, and also set up and maintain a sufficient light or sufficient lights during the whole of the night-time, to the satisfaction of the said Commissioners respectively, to prevent accidents and mischief happening therefrom : Provided always, that nothing herein contained shall interfere with or prejudice any power or authority now vested in the Mayor of the borough of *Newbury* for the time being, for regulating market carts and waggons on market days, but the same shall be as good valid and effectual as if this Act had not been passed.

54. And be it further Enacted, That if the drivers of any waggon, cart, car, dray or other carriage, shall ride upon any such carriage in any highway, market, street, square, way, lane, public passage or place within the said borough and town, or tithing or hamlet respectively, not having some other person on foot or on horseback to guide the same, (such carriages as are usually conducted by some person holding the reins of the horse or horses drawing the same excepted;) or if the driver of any carriage whatsoever shall in any such highways, market, street, square, way, lane, public passage or place, furiously drive the same, or shall by negligence or wilful misbehaviour cause any hurt or damage to any person or carriage, or shall wilfully be at such distance from such carriage whilst it shall be passing in any such highway, market, street, square, way, lane, public passage or place, that he cannot have the direction and government of the horse or horses or other cattle drawing the same; or shall by furious or overdriving the same, or by negligence or wilful misbehaviour, prevent, hinder or interrupt the free passage of any carriage, or of any of his Majesty's subjects in any such highways, market, street, square, way, lane, public passage or place; or if the driver, of any empty or unloaded waggon cart or other carriage shall refuse or neglect to turn aside and make way for any coach, chariot, chaise, loaded waggon, cart or other carriage, then and in every such case every such driver so offending, and being convicted of any such offence, either by his own confession, the view of a Justice of the peace, or by the oath of one or more credible witness or witnesses before any Justice of the peace for the county town or place where such offence shall be committed, shall for every such offence forfeit and pay any sum not exceeding five pounds, in case the driver shall not be the owner of

such carriage, and in case such driver be the owner of such carriage, then any sum not exceeding ten pounds; and every such driver offending in any of the said cases shall and may, by authority of this Act, with or without any warrant, be apprehended by any person or persons who shall see such offence committed; and it shall be lawful for the person or persons so apprehending such driver, to convey such driver, or to cause him to be conveyed or delivered to a constable or other peace officer, in order to be conveyed before some Justice of the peace for such county, town or place aforesaid, to be dealt with according to law; and if any such driver, in any of the cases aforesaid, shall refuse to disclose his name, it shall be lawful for the Justices of the peace to whom he shall be taken, or to whom such complaint shall be made, to commit him to the gaol for such county, town or place aforesaid for any time not exceeding three months, or to proceed against such offender for the penalty aforesaid, by a description of the person and the offence, and expressing in such proceedings that such driver refused to disclose his name.

55. And be it further Enacted, That whenever the pavements or flagging of any of the said markets, streets, squares, ways, lanes, public passages or places within the said borough and town, or tithing or hamlet respectively, shall be broken up for the making or repairing any vault drain or sewer, or for the purpose of laying altering or repairing any pipe or pipes, aqueduct or aqueducts, or any plug or plugs thereof, under the said markets, streets, squares, ways, lanes, public passages or places, or any of them, or for any other lawful purpose, the person or persons breaking up such pavements or flagging, or liable to the repair of such vault, drain, sewer, pipe, aqueduct or plug, and

the person or persons for whom or by whose order the same shall be so done, shall and he she or they is and are hereby required, at their own proper costs and charges, to make or repair such vault, drain, sewer, pipe, aqueduct, or plug without the least delay, and forthwith afterwards to relay amend and repair the pavement or flagging of the said market, street, square, way, lane, public passage or place so broken up, in a good substantial manner, to the satisfaction of the said Commissioners respectively, or the surveyor or surveyors appointed for the purposes of this Act; and in default thereof, it shall be lawful for the surveyor or surveyors to the said Commissioners respectively, or any person or persons acting by or under the authority of the said commissioners respectively, to repair amend and make good the market, street, square, way, lane, public passage or place so broken up, and the costs and charges shall be borne and paid by the person or persons by whom or by whose order such market, street, square, way, lane, public passage or place, or any part thereof, shall have been so broken up; and in default of payment thereof for seven days next after demand shall be made by such surveyor, or other person acting by or under the authority of the said Commissioners respectively, such costs and charges, together with any sum not exceeding ten shillings, by way of penalty, shall and may be levied and recovered in such and the like manner as any penalty can or may be levied and recovered by virtue of this Act from the person or persons so making default.

56. And be it further Enacted, That if any person or persons shall wilfully or maliciously break up, injure, destroy or otherwise damage any of the articles and things hereby vested in the said Commissioners respectively, or any of the works done by them in

pursuance of this Act, every person so offending shall for every such offence forfeit and pay any sum not exceeding five pounds, besides what shall be sufficient to repair such damage.

57. And be it further Enacted, That during the time any market, street, square, way, lane, public passage or place shall be new paving flagging or repairing, or any of the grates, drains, sewers, or other work therein shall be altering or repairing, the said Commissioners for their respective jurisdictions shall have power to order the necessary materials to be lodged in that or any adjoining market, street, square, way, lane, public passage or place, or markets, streets, squares, ways, lanes, public passages or places according to their discretion, as also to stop up the way through that or any adjacent market, street, square, way, lane, public passage or place, so long as they shall judge necessary, and the said Commissioners respectively, and all persons acting under the directions of the said Commissioners respectively, are hereby indemnified from any prosecution or action whatsoever for so doing.

58. And be it further Enacted, That it shall be lawful for the said Commissioners for their respective jurisdictions from time to time to appoint such and so many paviours, artificers, workmen, labourers, carters and others, and also to purchase any horses, carts, tools, implements and materials, as they shall judge necessary for the purpose of carrying this Act into execution.

59. And be it further Enacted, That the said Commissioners for their respective jurisdictions shall have full power to purchase or rent lands, so that such lands for each district do not exceed half an acre, for

depositing the stone and other materials for the
several purposes of this Act, and for depositing dirt,
dung, soil, ashes, cinders and rubbish, and the
purchase-money or rent thereof shall be paid out of
the money or fund raised or to be raised for paving,
widening, amending, cleansing, watering, extending
and regulating the markets, streets, squares, ways,
lanes, public passages and places by virtue of this
Act, and the property thereof shall be and is hereby
vested in the said Commissioners respectively for the
purposes of this Act.

60. And be it further Enacted, That it shall be
lawful for the said Commissioners for their respective
jurisdictions to take down, remove, alter or regulate,
in such manner as they shall from time to time judge
proper, all signs and other emblems used to denote
the trade occupation or calling of any person or
persons, and all signs, sign irons, sign posts and
other posts, sheds, penthouses, spouts, gutters, steps,
stairs, cellar doors, cellar lids, bow and other projecting windows, window shutters, window flaps, stumps,
trees, rails, pails, pasiladoes, porchers, bulks, show
glasses and show boards, pools, cesspools, cisterns and
reservoirs for water, and other encroachments projections and annoyances belonging to, or which shall
hereafter be affixed or belong to any house or houses
or other buildings, or which shall in any other way be
placed or fixed, and which do or in the judgment of
the said Commissioners respectively obstruct the free
and commodious passage along the carriage or footways of any of the said markets, squares, streets,
ways, lanes, public passages or places of or within
the said borough and town, or tithing or hamlet respectively; and also to cause the water to be conveyed from the roofs, cornices, eaves and penthouses
of or belonging to such houses or other buildings re-

spectively, by proper pipes or trunks to be affixed to the sides of such houses or other buildings respectively, and to be brought down to the ground, and the costs, charges, and expenses attending the taking down, taking away, removing, altering or regulating such signs, sign irons, sign posts and other posts, sheds, penthouses, spouts, gutters, steps, stairs, cellar doors, cellar lids, bow or other projecting windows, window shutters, window flaps, stumps, trees, rails, pales, palisadoes, porchers, bulks, show glasses, show boards, pools, cesspools, cisterns and reservoirs for water, and other encroachments projections and annoyances, or any of them, and of making and affixing such pipes or trunks as aforesaid, shall be borne and defrayed out of the money to be raised by virtue of this Act.

61.   And be it further Enacted, That if any house or other building in or near any market, square, street, way, lane or other public passage or place within the said borough and town, or tithing or hamlet respectively, shall after the passing of this Act be made erected or built in such manner and form as in the front or in any of the gables or sides thereof to project into or over such market, square, street, way, lane or other public passage or place, or in any other manner or form than in a perpendicular line or direction upwards from the foundation of such house or building; or if any spout pipe or trunk for conveying water from the roofs eaves or cornices or any house or other building in any market, square, street, way, lane, public passage or place in the said borough and town, or tithing or hamlet respectively, shall be fixed otherwise than from the roof eaves or cornices thereof by such spouts pipes or trunks on the front sides of such houses or buildings respectively, and brought down to the ground ; or if any sign, sign iron, sign post or other post, shed, penthouse, step, stair, bow window

or other projecting window, window shutter, window
flap, stump, rail, palisado, porch, bulk, show glass,
show board, pool, cesspool, cistern or reservoir for
water, or any other encroachment or projection
against or in front or outside of any house or other
building within or adjoining to any market, square,
street, lane, public passage or place within the said
borough and town, or tithing or hamlet respectively,
shall be made erected or built so as to obstruct the free
and commodious passage along the carriage or footways of the same, then and in every such case the
owner and owners of every such house or other
building, sign, sign iron, sign post or other post, shed,
penthouse, step, stair, bow or other projecting
windows, window shutter, window flap, stump, rail,
pale, palisado, porch, bulk, show glass, show board,
pool, cesspool, cistern or reservoir for water, or other
encroachment or projection which shall be so made
erected or built as aforesaid, or of any such spout,
pipe or trunk which shall be so made or affixed otherwise than aforesaid, contrary to this Act, shall for
every such offence forfeit and pay any sum not exceeding ten shillings a day for every day such house
or other building, sign, sign iron, sign post or other
post, shed, penthouse, step, stair, bow or other projecting window, window shutter, window flap, stump,
rail, pale, palisado, porch, bulk, show glass, show
board, pool, cesspool, cistern or reservoir for water,
spout, pipe or trunk, or other encroachment or projection shall continue in such state, shall be contrary
to the provisions and directions of this Act; and it
shall be lawful for the said Commissioners for their
respective jurisdictions (whether any such penalties
or forfeitures shall be levied or not,) to cause all
such houses or other buildings, signs, sign irons, sign
posts, sheds, penthouses, steps, stairs, bow windows
or other projecting windows, window shutters, window

flaps, stumps, trees, rails, pales, palisadoes, porches, bulks, show glasses, show boards, pools, cesspools, cisterns and reservoirs for water, spouts, pipes, trunks, and other encroachments and projections, or any of them, to be taken down removed and taken away.

62. And be it further Enacted, That where any bulk, post, porch, or other projection or obstruction, shall be removed by authority of this Act, for the purpose of widening or altering any market, street, square, way, lane, or other public passage or place within the said borough and town, and for or in respect of which any annual sum or sums hath or have been usually paid by way of quit rent, fee-farm rent, or other acknowledgement, to any person or persons, body or bodies politic or corporate, then and in every such case such annual sum or sums of money shall cease to be any longer paid or payable, and shall be considered as absolutely extinguished : Provided always, that the said Commissioners for their respective jurisdictions shall in every such case make such satisfaction and compensation to the person or persons, body or bodies politic or corporate, to whom any annual sum or sums hath or have been paid as aforesaid, by the payment of a gross sum or sums of money out of the monies to be raised by virtue of this Act, as the said Commissioners respectively shall judge to be of the value of the annual sum or sums so paid ; and in case of any difference or dispute between the said Commissioners respectively, and any such person or persons, body or bodies politic or corporate, respecting the sum or sums of money so to be paid by the said Commissioners respectively, as a satisfaction and compensation for any such quit rent fee-farm rent, or other acknowledgement as aforesaid, such satisfaction and compensation shall be settled and ascertained in such and the like manner as the

satisfaction and compensation to be made by the said
Commissioners respectively, for the purchase of any
lands, tenements or hereditaments for the purposes
of this Act are herein directed to be ascertained and
settled; and such sum and sums of money, when so
settled and ascertained, shall be paid to or disposed
of for the use and benefit of the party or parties
entitled thereto, in such and the like manner as any
sum or sums of money to be paid for the purchase of
any lands, tenements or hereditaments by the said
Commissioners respectively is and are herein directed
to be paid or disposed of: Provided always, that if
the said Commissioners for their respective jurisdictions shall cause to be taken up or removed any
stumps, post or other guards at the corner of any
house or building, forming a corner of any street or
lane for the protection of such house from injury by
carriages, they the said Commissioners respectively
shall, by some other proper ways or means sufficiently
guard or protect the same from damage as aforesaid;
and in case any damage shall at any time happen to
any such house by reason of taking up or removing
any such stumps, posts or other guards by the said
Commissioners respectively, they the said Commissioners respectively shall from time to time make
good such damage out of the monies to be raised by
virtue of this Act, for paving and repairing the
streets of the said borough and town, and tithing or
hamlet respectively.

63. And be it further Enacted, That it shall be
lawful for the said Commissioners respectively, and
they are hereby authorized and empowered from time
to time to cause to be cut made or laid in, through,
over, or under any of the present or future public
streets, lanes, roads, passages and places of the said
borough and town, or tithing or hamlet respectively,

any new tunnels, gutters, grates, sinks, drains, ditches, sewers, pipes, aqueducts or water courses, and also from time to time to cause any of the present or any future tunnels, gutters, grates, sinks, drains, ditches, sewers, pipes, aqueducts and watercourses, or any part or parts thereof respectively, to be stopped up, opened, scoured, cleansed, widened, straightened or deepened, or the form of line thereof to be turned, altered, varied or changed within any of such public streets, lanes, roads, passages or places, or under any houses, buildings or premises therein or thereto adjoining, in such manner as they the said Commissioners shall think fit, consistently with the provisions of this Act.

64. And be it further Enacted, That where any opening is now or may be made in the paving or flagging of any of the said markets, streets, squares, ways, lanes, public passages or places, as an entrance into, or for the purpose of conveying coals or other articles into any vault or cellar, whether such vault or cellar be inhabited or uninhabited, or for the purpose of conveying light into any room or cellar, or for any other purpose, the door, lid or lids, flap or flaps, covering or grating to such opening, shall be made at the expense of the person or persons repairing the same, and shall be made of iron or such other materials, of such dimensions, and in such manner and form as the said Commissioners for their respective jurisdictions shall direct and approve of, and every such door, lid, flap, grating and covering, shall from time to time be repaired, varied and altered at the like expense of the person or persons for whose use and benefit the same shall be possessed and enjoyed, and in such manner and form as the said Commissioners respectively shall direct or appoint; and in case any person or persons shall neglect or refuse to make, repair, vary, or alter

such grating or covering, according to such direction or appointment as aforesaid, or shall cause or permit any such cellar door, cellar lid, flap or cover, within the said borough and town, or tithing or hamlet respectively, to be left open or not properly secured, at any time between sun-setting in the afternoon and sun-rising in the morning, on any pretence whatsoever, without the same being well and sufficiently lighted and guarded, or shall at any time permit the same to be or remain not properly fastened or secured, so as to prevent accidents from happening, every such person shall for every such offence forfeit and pay any sum not exceeding ten shillings, as also any further sum not exceeding twenty shillings, for every week the said offence shall be continued.

65. And be it further Enacted, That it shall be lawful for the said Commissioners for their respective jurisdictions, and they are hereby required to nominate and appoint any person or persons, and to purchase or hire any cart or carts, or other carriage or carriages, and also any horse or horses, for the purpose of cleansing and watering the several markets, streets, squares, ways, lanes, public passages or places within the said borough and town, or tithing or hamlet respectively, and of carrying away the dust, dung, manure, dirt and soil thereof; and it shall be lawful for the said Commissioners respectively to contract with any person or persons for cleansing and watering the same, and for carrying away the dust, dung, manure, dirt and soil thereof, upon such terms as they shall deem necessary, and to do and perform every act for carrying such contract into complete execution.

66. And be it further Enacted, That the person or persons employed by or contracting with the said

Commissioners for their respective jurisdictions for cleansing the several markets, streets, squares, ways, lanes, public passages and places within the said borough and town, and tithing or hamlet respectively, or the person or persons employed by or acting under the direction of such person or persons so contracting with the said Commissioners respectively, shall once in every week, (that is to say,) on every *Friday* between such hours of the day, and also on such other days at or between such hours as the Commissioners respectively aforesaid shall from time to time appoint, sweep and collect together all dirt, dust, manure, filth or rubbish in such markets, streets, squares, ways, lanes, public passages and places, and shall also bring, or cause to be brought, a cart or other proper carriage into such markets, streets, squares, ways, lanes, public passages and places where such cart or other carriage can pass, and shall at his or their approach with such cart or other carriage, and not before, by sound of bell, voice or otherwise, give notice to the inhabitants of his or their coming, and give the like notice in every court passage or place into which such cart or carriage cannot pass, and such person or persons aforesaid shall immediately take the dust, dirt, manure, rubbish, cinders, ashes and other filth (except filth from any privy or necessary-house) from the respective premises in such several markets, streets, squares, ways, lanes, public passages and places, and put the same into such cart or carriage: all which dust, dirt, manure, rubbish, cinders, ashes, and filth, (except as aforesaid,) as well as all such dirt, dung, ashes, and other filth as shall be swept up and collected together as aforesaid, such person or persons shall then immediately, or as soon as may be, carry away or cause to be carried away to the place or places appointed for depositing the same, upon pain of forfeiting any sum not exceeding forty shillings for every offence or neglect therein; and the person or persons so employed as aforesaid shall cause the words " Scavengers Cart", to be painted in large Roman letters, at least one inch in length each, on the front or some other conspicuous part of every cart or carriage used for the purposes aforesaid, on pain of forfeiting any sum not exceeding ten shillings for every neglect therein; and if any such person employed as aforesaid shall sweep or throw away any dust, dirt manure, ashes or filth into any drain, sewer, sink or watercourse within the said borough and town, or tithing or hamlet respectively, every person so offending shall for every such offence forfeit and pay any sum not exceeding twenty shillings.

67. And be it further Enacted, That if any person or persons whomsoever, other than the person or persons employed by or contracting with the said Commissioners for their respective jurisdictions for cleansing the several markets, streets, squares, ways, lanes, public passages or places within the said borough and town, and tithing or hamlet respectively, or the person or persons employed by or acting under the direction of the person or persons so contracting as aforesaid, shall take and carry away, or cause to be taken and carried away any dust, dung, manure, dirt, ashes or other filth out of any such markets, streets, squares, ways, lanes, or other public passages or places as aforesaid, every such person so offending shall for every such offence forfeit and pay any sum not exceeding twenty shillings.

68. Provided always, and be it further Enacted, That nothing herein contained shall extend or be construed to extend to any ashes, cinders, dust, dirt, manure, filth, soil, dung or rubbish, which any of the

inhabitants of the said borough and town, and tithing or hamlet respectively, shall have occasion and think fit to preserve and keep within their own respective houses, yards gardens and premises, but the same shall respectively belong to and be at the disposal of the person or persons so reserving the name, so as such ashes, cinders, dust, dirt, manure, filth, soil, dung or rubbish be not laid down or placed in any of the said markets, streets, squares, ways, lanes, public passages or places in the said borough and town, or tithing or hamlet respectively, for any longer time than shall be necessary for the loading and carrying away the same, and so as the same do not annoy the neighbour or neighbours of such person or persons, nor the public in general; and in case such person or persons so reserving such ashes, cinders, dust, dirt, manure, filth, soil, dung or rubbish, shall wilfully or negligently permit or suffer the same to lie in any of the said markets, streets, squares, ways, lanes, public passages or places in the said borough and town, or tithing or hamlet respectively, for any longer time than three hours for the purpose of loading and carrying away the same, or shall suffer the same to annoy his or their neighbours, or the public in general, or permit or suffer the soil or contents of any privy or necessary-house to remain in any of the said markets, streets, squares, ways, lanes, public passages and places after the hour of six in the morning, such peror persons shall for every such offence forfeit and pay any sum not exceeding forty shillings; and it shall be lawful for the person or persons to be appointed by or contracting with the said Commissioners for their respective jurisdictions for cleansing the said markets, streets, squares, ways, lanes, public passages and places, and they are hereby authorized and directed to take and convert such ashes, cinders, dust, dirt, manure, filth, soil, dung and rubbish to his or their

own use and uses, and to sell and dispose of the same
without rendering any satisfaction for the same.

69. And be it further Enacted, That the respective
occupiers of houses or other buildings, with the appurtenances, within the several markets, streets,
squares, ways, lanes, public passages and places within
the said borough and town or tithing or hamlet respectively, the churchwardens and chapelwardens of
every church and chapel, or any one or more of them,
the owner and owners and proprietor and proprietors
of every dead wall and vacant piece of land, or
any one or more of them, the proprietor and proprietors, trustee and trustees, treasurer and minister
of every meeting-house or other place of public
worship, or any one or more of them, and the person
and persons who for the time being shall be the os-
tensible director or directors, manager or managers of
every hospital, prison, school, and other public building respectively, situate or being in the several
markets, streets, squares, ways, lanes, public passages
and places within the said borough and town, or
tithing or hamlet respectively, shall and they are
hereby required to cause to be well and sufficiently
swept and cleansed the footways and foot-pavements
the whole length of the front of their respective houses,
buildings, churches and churchyards, chapel and
chapelyards, dead walls, vacant pieces of ground,
meeting-houses, hospitals, prisons, schools and other
public buildings, tenements, yards, gardens or other
hereditaments, and the channels and watercourses
opposite the same respectively, to the full extent of
the said footways and foot-pavements, before behind
and on the side or sides of the same respectively,
previous to the hour of nine of the clock in the
morning, on every *Wednesday*, and *Friday* in every
week, and oftener, on such other days, and at such

other times, if the said Commissioners for their respective jurisdictions shall from time to time order or
require the same, and shall also cause the dirt and soil
to arise from such sweeping and cleansing to be collected and put together (so as not to obstruct either
the carriage or footway, or the channel or watercourse
ias aforesaid,) in order that the same may be removed
by the said scavenger or other person to be employed
for that purpose, upon pain of forfeiting any sum
not exceeding five shillings for every neglect
therein. '

70. And be it further Enacted, That if any sort
of cattle or swine shall at any time be found wandering about any of the markets, streets, squares, ways,
lanes, or other public passages or places within the
said borough and town, or tithing or hamlet respectively, the owner or owners thereof shall for every
such head of cattle or swine forfeit and pay any sum
not exceeding ten shillings ; and moreover, it shall
be lawful for any person or persons appointed by the
said Commissioners for their respective jurisdictions,
if he or they shall think proper, to seize and impound
such cattle or swine in the common pound of the
said borough and town, or tithing or hamlet respectively, or in such other place as the said Commissioners
respectively shall appoint, and the same there to remain until the owner or owners thereof shall for every
such head of cattle or swine so impounded pay the
sum of five shillings to the person impounding the
same, together with the reasonable charges and expenses of impounding and keeping the same ; and in
case the said sum charges and expenses shall not be
paid within four days after such impounding, it shall
be lawful for the said Commissioners respectively to
sell or cause to be sold the same, and the money
arising from such sale, after deducting the said sum

of five shillings, and the charges and expenses of impounding, keeping and selling such cattle or swine, shall be paid to the person or persons whose property the cattle or swine so sold shall appear to have been.

71. And be it further Enacted, That in case any person or persons shall release or attempt to release any cattle or swine, which shall be seized for the purpose of being impounded under the authority of this Act, from the pound or place where the same shall be so impounded, or shall pull down damage or destroy the same pound or place, or any part thereof, or any lock or bolt belonging thereto, or with which the same shall be fastened, or shall rescue or release or attempt to rescue or release any distress or levy which shall be made under the authority of this Act, until or before such cattle or swine seized or so impounded, or such distress or levy so made shall be discharged by due course of law, every person so offending shall upon conviction thereof before any one of His Majesty's Justices of the peace for the county town or place where the offence shall be committed, either on confession of the party or parties offending, or upon the oath of one credible witness, (and which oath the said Justice is hereby authorized and empowered to administer,) to be committed by such Justice, by warrant under his hand and seal, to the common gaol or house of correction of the said county town or place, there to remain without bail or mainprize for any time not exceeding three calendar months.

72. And be it further Enacted, That it shall be lawful for the said Commissioners for their respective jurisdictions, and they are hereby authorized and empowered from time to time, and at any time or

times after passing this Act, to purchase and provide
such and so many glass lamps of such sorts and sizes,
and such and so many lamp irons and lamp posts, and
all such other matters and things for lighting such
lamps, either by oil or gas or otherwise, as they shall
judge necessary; and to direct the same to be affixed
and set up on or against the walls or palisadoes of all
or any of the houses tenements or buildings, or
against any other walls, or for supplying such lamps
with oil, gas or otherwise, under any of the markets,
streets, squares, ways, lanes public passages and
places within the said borough and town, or tithing
or hamlet respectively, or in any other manner they
shall think proper and convenient, and to be taken
down, altered or removed when and as often as they
shall think fit; and to cause such lamps, or any of
them, to be lighted at such seasons of the year, on
such evenings, in such manner and at such hours of
the evening, and to be kept burning for so many
hours as to them the said Commissioners respectively
shall seem necessary or proper for the well and
sufficient lighting of all or any of the said markets,
streets, squares, ways, lanes, public passages and
places within the said borough and town, or tithing
or hamlet respectively : Provided always, that it shall
be lawful for the said Commissioners respectively to
make any contract or authorize the making of any contract or contracts for the lighting the said borough
and town, or tithing or hamlet respectively with gas,
and to prepare or permit the preparing, or lay down
or prepare the laying down of all necessary iron pipes
or reservoirs, or matters or things, necessary for the
lighting of the said borough and town, or tithing or
hamlet respectively with gas : Provided always,
that nothing herein contained shall authorize or
empower the said Commissioners respectively, or
any other person or persons, to carry lay or fix, or

continue any pipe or pipes, or any other thing for the conveyance of the said gas or inflammable air, through or against any dwelling-house or private building, or any private lands, hereditaments or premises, without the consent of the owner and occupier thereof respectively for that purpose; provided also, that if any injury or damage shall be occasioned to any rail, palisado, building or wall, by the affixing, setting up, taking down, altering or removing any such lamp or lamps, or any lamp iron or lamp irons, or other fastener thereof, the Commissioners respectively shall immediately cause the said injury and damage to be well and sufficiently repaired out of the money to be raised within their respective jurisdictions by virtue of this Act.

73. And be it further Enacted, That if any person or persons shall wilfully break, take away, throw down or otherwise destroy or damage any lamp or lamps already erected or which shall be erected by order of the said Commissioners for their respective jurisdictions, or by the said Mayor, Aldermen and Burgesses, or their successors, or by any person or persons at his her or their own expense, for the purpose of lighting any of the said markets, streets, squares, ways, lanes, public passages and places, or any post, iron, cover or other furniture thereof, or shall wilfully extinguish the light or lights of any lamp or lamps, it shall be lawful for any Justice of the peace for the county town or place where the offence shall be committed, and he is hereby required upon complaint to him made by any one or more credible witness or witnesses of any such offence, to issue a warrant for apprehending the party or parties accused; or it shall be lawful for any person or persons who shall see such offence committed to apprehend, and also for any person or persons to assist in apprehending the offender or offenders, and by

authority of this Act, without any other warrant, to deliver him or them into the custody of a peace officer, in order to be secured and conveyed before some Justice of the peace of the county town or place aforesaid, and on the party or parties accused being brought before such Justice, such Justice shall proceed to examine upon oath any witness or witnesses who shall appear to be produced to give evidence touching such offence; and if the party or parties accused shall be convicted of such offence, either by his her or their confession, or upon such evidence as aforesaid, then and in every such case he she or they shall for each and every such offence respectively, and if more than one shall severally forfeit and pay any sum not exceeding five pounds, and shall besides make a full satisfaction (to be ascertained by such Justice) to the said Commissioners respectively, or other party injured, for the damage so done; and in case such offender or offenders shall not, upon conviction, forthwith pay such penalty by him her or them incurred, and also such satisfaction as aforesaid, such Justice is hereby required to commit such offender or offenders to the gaol of the county town or place aforesaid, there to be kept to hard labour for any time not exceeding six calendar months, unless such penalty and satisfaction as aforesaid shall be sooner paid.

74. And be it further Enacted, That if any person or persons shall carelessly negligently or accidentally break, throw down or otherwise destroy or damage any such lamp or lamps so being hung out or set up as aforesaid, or any post, iron, cover or furniture thereof respectively, and shall not upon demand make satisfaction for the damage so done, then and in every such case it shall be lawful for any Justice of the peace for the county town or place wherein the offence shall be committed, and he is hereby required, upon com-

plaint thereof made by one or more credible witness or witnesses, by warrant under his hand to summon before him the party or parties complained of for doing such damage, and upon his, her or their appearing, or making default to appear (oath being made that the party complained against had being served with such summons, or that the same had been left at his her or their usual dwelling or place of abode if known, or that he she or they could not be found,) such Justice shall proceed to examine the cause of such complaint, and upon proof thereof, either upon confession of the party or the oath of one or more witness or witnesses, shall award and order such satisfaction to be made by the party or parties complained against, for the damage so done to the said Commissioners respectively, or other owner or owners of such lamp or lamps, as to such Justice shall appear just and reasonable ; and in case the sum so awarded shall not be paid forthwith, it shall and may be lawful to and for such Justice, and he is hereby required to cause the same to be levied and recovered as any fine or penalty can or may be levied by virtue of this Act.

75. Provided also, and be it further Enacted, That for the greater security against accidents by such gas works, the said Commissioners for their respective jurisdictions, and all other persons with whom they may contract, are hereby directed and required to erect or cause to be erected all such gasometers, cisterns, pillars, and all other the necessary apparatus, and to lay all such pipes, stopcocks, syphons, plugs, branches and machinery as aforesaid, by the advice and direction of some person or persons, thoroughly skilled and experienced in the nature of such works, whose entire approbation thereof as to safety and otherwise shall be had before the same shall be used for the purposes of this Act.

76. And be it further Enacted, That the said Commissioners for their respective jurisdictions, and the person or persons with whom they shall contract, shall and they are hereby required to have the said works inspected at least twice in every year by one or more experienced person or persons, to see that the same are in a fit state, and properly conducted and managed; and in case of any error, want of repair, insufficiency, or other mismanagement being pointed out, to cause the same to be forthwith corrected, amended and repaired according to the opinion of such person or persons.

77. And be it further Enacted, That in case the said Commissioners for their respective jurisdictions shall deem it expedient to erect such gas apparatus, and to light the said markets, streets, squares, ways, lanes, and other public passages and places, or any of them, with gas or inflammable air, without contracting for the same as aforesaid, it shall be lawful for the said Commissioners respectively, after sufficiently lighting the said markets, streets, squares, ways, lanes, and other public passages and places, to let out or grant to any person or persons whomsoever, who shall be willing to take the same, any light or lights, or argand, cockspur, batwing, or any other kind of burner or burners, and to supply the same with gas or inflammable air upon such terms and conditions, and at such annual rents for the same, and in such manner as they the said Commissioners respectively shall from time to time think proper; and for that purpose to direct the breaking up of the pavement and soil thereof, and do all other things that may be necessary for furnishing and conveying any such light or lights as aforesaid: Provided nevertheless, that all monies to proceed therefrom or arise thereby be in the first instance applied to defray the

H

expense of the gas apparatus, and other things connected therewith ; and if there by any overplus, then
the same shall be applied generally for the purposes
of this Act within the respective jurisdictions of the
said Commissioners.

78. And be it further Enacted, That in case any
person or persons who shall contract with the said
Commissioners for their respective jurisdictions, or
otherwise agree to take, or shall use and enjoy the
benefit of the said gas in his, her or their private
dwellings, warehouses, shops, inns, taverns, or other
buildings, or manufactories, shall refuse or neglect ·
for the space of seven days after demand thereof
made by the said Commissioners respectively, or by
any person under their authority, to pay the sum or
sums of money then due for the same to the said
Commissioners respectively, according to the terms
and stipulations of the said Commissioners respectively, it shall be lawful for the said Commissioners
respectively, or their clerk, or any person or persons
acting by or under their authority, by warrant under
the hand and seal of any Justice of the peace for
the county town or place wherein the offence shall be
committed, to levy the said sum or sums of money,
in respect whereof such neglect or refusal shall
happen, by distress and sale of the goods and chattels
of the person or persons so neglecting or refusing to
pay the same, rendering the overplus (if any) to such
person or persons so refusing or neglecting after the
necessary charges of making such distress and sale
be first deducted.

79. And be it further Enacted, That the branch
or service pipes which shall be put down for lighting
the said markets, streets, squares, ways, lanes, and
other public passages and places, shall be kept fully

charged with gas, and the stop cocks shall be so turned as not to impede or prevent the said branch or service pipes being completely filled with gas during the time the same shall be lighted.

80. And be it further Enacted, That all and every the pipes or other conduits to be laid or used for the conveyance of gas in, under, through, along, across or round any market, street, square, way, lane, or other passage or place within the limits of this Act, shall be so laid at the greatest practicable distance, and whenever the width of the carriageway in such street or place will allow thereof, at the distance of three feet at least from the nearest part of any water pipe, sough, or watercourse already laid down, or hereafter to be laid down, for the conveyance of water in, under, through, along, across or around any of the said markets, streets, squares, ways, lanes, or other passages or places within the limits of this Act, except in cases where it shall be unavoidably necessary to lay the gas pipes across any of the said water pipes, soughs, or watercourses, in which cases the said gas pipes shall be laid over and above the said water pipes, soughs and watercourses, at the greatest practical distance therefrom, and shall form therewith a right angle, and in such cases the said gas pipes so crossing the said water pipes, soughs and watercourses shall be at least three feet in length, so that no joint or any of the said gas pipes shall be nearer to any part of the said water pipes, soughs or watercourses than three feet at least; and in laying down the said gas pipes the said Commissioners respectively, contractors, or other persons supplying gas, shall in no case join three or more gas pipes together previous to their being laid in the trench, but shall lay each pipe as near as may be in its place in the trench, and shall in such trench properly form the jointing with the

other pipes to be added thereto with proper and sufficient materials: and shall also make and keep all and every such pipes, and all pipes connected or communicating therewith, and all the screws, joints, inlets, apertures or openings therein respectively air-tight, and in all and every respect prevent the said gas from escaping therefrom, upon pain of forfeiting, for every offence, the sum of five pounds.

81. And be it further Enacted, That whenever any gas shall be found to escape from any of the pipes which shall be laid down or set up in pursuance of this Act, the said Commissioners for their respective jurisdictions, or the body or bodies politic or corporate, or any person or persons contracting to light or lighting with gas the said markets, streets, squares, ways, lanes, and other public passages and places, or any house or building therein, shall immediately after notice given to them or him, by parol or in writing, of any such escape of gas from any person or persons whomsoever, cause the most speedy and effectual measures to be taken to stop and prevent such gas from escaping; and in case the said Commissioners respectively, or the body or bodies politic or corporate, or person or persons so lighting with gas, shall not within twenty-four hours next after such notice given effectually stop and prevent any future escape, and wholly and satis-factorily remove the cause of complaint, then and in every such case the said Commissioners respectively, or the body and bodies, politic or corporate, or person or persons as aforesaid, shall for every such offence forfeit and pay any sum not exceeding five pounds for each day after the expiration of twenty-four hours from the time of giving any such notice, during which the gas shall be suffered to escape as aforesaid; which penalty or penalties shall from time to time be re-coverable in a summary way, on the oath of one or

more credible witness or witnesses, by information to be laid before some one or more Justice or Justices of the peace for the county town or place wherein the offence shall be committed, and shall and may be recoverable and levied, with all reasonable charges, by distress and sale of the goods and chattels, of the treasurer of the said Commissioners respectively, or of the goods and chattels of the body or bodies politic or corporate, or of the person or persons lighting as aforesaid.

82.   And be it further Enacted, That if any person or persons shall wilfully or maliciously remove, take away, destroy, damage or injure any part of any pipe, plug, post or other apparatus, article matter or thing, belonging to the said Commissioners for their respective jurisdictions, or to any body or bodies politic or corporate, or person or persons lighting as aforesaid, or shall wilfully and maliciously waste, or beyond his her or their contract consume any of the inflammable air or gas supplied by the said Commissioners respectively, or any body or bodies politic or corporate, or person or persons as aforesaid, every person so offending in any of the respective premises, and being thereof lawfully convicted, either by confession or on the oath or affirmation of one credible witness before one or more Justice or Justices of the peace for the county town or place wherein the offence shall be committed, shall forfeit and pay to the said Commissioners respectively, or the body or bodies politic or corporate, or person or persons aforesaid, any sum not exceeding five pounds, and three times the amount of the damage done or occasioned by such conduct, the same to be ascertained by such Justice or Justices: and such penalty and damage, together with reasonable costs, shall be levied by distress and sale of the goods and chattels of such offender, returning the

overplus (if any) on demand to the owner of such goods and chattels, or such offender shall and may be committed to the gaol of the county town or place aforesaid, at the discretion of such Justice or Justices, there to remain for any time not exceeding three calendar months.

83. And be it further Enacted, That it shall not be lawful for the said Commissioners respectively, or body or bodies politic or corporate, or any person or persons whomsoever, to carry or convey, or cause to be carried or conveyed any washings or liquids, or any lime or other ingredients, matters or things whatsoever, which shall arise or be made in manufacturing or preparing any gas or inflammable air whatsoever, or in the prosecution of any of the gas works, into the river *Kennet*, or into any pond, ditch, brook or canal, or any sewer, drain, conduit or other place whatsoever, by which it may ultimately be carried or conveyed into the said river, or into any other stream or brooks, or into any pond, ditch, brook, canal, sewer, drain or conduit.

84. Provided always and be it further Enacted, That if the said Commissioners for their respective jurisdictions, or body or bodies politic or corporate, or any person or persons, whosoever making furnishing or supplying any gas, used burnt or consumed for lighting any street highway or place, or any building manufactory or other premises within the limits of this Act, shall at any time drain or carry, or cause or suffer to be drained carried or conveyed, or to run or flow, any washings or other waste liquids, substances or things whatsoever, which shall arise or be made in the prosecution of any gas works, into the river *Kennet*, or into any river brook or running stream, reservoir, canal, aqueduct, waterway, feeder, pond or

springhead, or do or cause to be done any annoyance act or thing to the water contained in such river, brook or running stream, reservoir, canal, aqueduct, waterway, feeder, pond, or springhead, whereby the said water or any part thereof shall or may be soiled, fouled, or corrupted, then and in every such case the said Commissioners respectively, or such body or bodies politic or corporate, or such person or persons as aforesaid, shall forfeit and pay for every such offence the sum of two hundred pounds; and such penalty or forfeiture shall and may be sued for and recovered, together with full costs of suit, in any of His Majesty's courts of record at Westminster, by action of debt or on the case, or by bill, plaint or information, wherein no essoign, protection, privilege, wager of law, nor more than one imparlance, shall be allowed, and such penalty shall be paid to the person or persons who shall inform or sue for the same: Provided always, that no such penalty or forfeiture shall be recovered unless the same be sued for within six calendar months after the time such annoyance act and thing shall have ceased; provided also, that in addition to the said penalty of two hundred pounds (and whether such penalty shall or shall not be recovered,) in case any of the said washings or other waste liquids, or noisome or offensive liquids substances or things, shall be drained conducted or conveyed, or caused or suffered to run or flow in manner aforesaid, into the said river *Kennet,* or into any river, brook, or running stream, or any reservoir, canal, aqueduct, waterway, feeder, pond, or spring-head, or any such annoyance act or thing shall be done or caused to be done as aforesaid, and notice thereof in writing shall have been given by any person whomsoever to the said Commissioners for their respective jurisdictions, or any of them, or to such body or bodies politic or corporate, or person or persons as aforesaid, and the said Commissioners respectively, or such body politic or corporate, or other person or persons, shall not within twenty-four hours after such notice given stop and prevent all and every such washings, waste liquids, or noisome and offensive liquids, substances or things, from being drained, conducted or conveyed, or from running or flowing in manner aforesaid, and every such other annoyance act or thing from being done as aforesaid, then and in every such case the said Commissioners respectively, or body or bodies politic or corporate, or other person or persons, shall forfeit and pay the sum of twenty pounds for each day such washings, waste liquids, or noisome or offensive liquids or things shall be so drained, conducted or conveyed, or caused or suffered to run or flow in manner aforesaid, or such other annoyance, act or thing shall be so done or caused to be done as aforesaid; and such last mentioned penalty shall and may be recovered and levied and shall be paid to the informer, or to the person or persons who in the judgment of the Justice or Justices before whom the conviction shall take place shall have sustained any annoyance injury or damage by any such act so done or committed.

85. Provided always, and be it further Enacted, That nothing herein contained shall extend or be construed to extend to prevent any person or persons from proceeding by indictment or otherwise against the said Commissioners, or the body or bodies politic or corporate, or the person or persons whosoever making, furnishing or supplying any gas used burnt or consumed for lighting any street, highway or place, or any building, manufactory or other premises within the limits of this Act, or their respective officers, servants or workmen, in respect of any public or private nuisance by them committed through the

means which shall be adopted in obtaining, making, preparing or using the said gas or inflammable air.

86. And be it further Enacted, That it shall be lawful for the said Commissioners for their respective jurisdictions to erect or build, or cause to be erected and built, one or more fire-engine house or houses within the said borough and town or tithing or hamlet respectively, and to provide one or more fire-engine or engines, together with all such pipes, buckets, and other articles and things, as may be necessary for working and using the same, and to defray the expenses thereof out of the rates to be raised by virtue of this Act.

87. And be it further Enacted, That it shall be lawful for the said Commissioners for the said borough and town, or any five or more of them, and they are hereby authorized and empowered, to build and erect, or cause to be built and erected, on any lands, tenements, hereditaments, and premises, to be purchased for the purposes of this Act, a convenient town-hall, gaol and butchers shambles, with suitable and proper rooms, out-offices and other appurtenances thereto, and also such proper house or place for the residence of the gaoler or keeper of the said gaol, to be fitted up and furnished respectively, in a complete and effectual manner as to them the said Commissioners, or any five or more of them, shall seem best adapted to answer the several uses for which the same are respectively appointed; and the same shall be conveyed to the said mayor, aldermen and burgesses, and their successors, who are hereby authorized to hold the same in perpetual succession for the purposes hereinbefore mentioned.

88. And be it further Enacted, That it shall be

lawful for the said Commissioners for their respective jurisdictions to contract and agree with any person or persons, body or bodies politic, corporate, collegiate or sole, as shall be or be deemed to be the owner or owners, proprietor or proprietors, or otherwise interested in any buildings, lands, tenements or hereditaments, within the said borough and town, or tithing or hamlet respectively, mentioned and specified in the Schedule to this Act annexed, for the absolute purchase in fee simple of any buildings, lands, tenements or hereditaments, or of any door or doors of any cellar or cellars, or of any steps belonging thereto, or in any other building whatsoever, which the said Commissioners respectively shall judge necessary and proper to be purchased for the purpose of opening, improving, and widening any markets, streets, lanes, roads, public passages or places within the said borough and town, or tithing or hamlet respectively, and also for enlarging the church yard belonging to the parish church of *Newbury*, aforesaid, or for the purpose of opening any communication between any markets, squares, streets, ways, lanes, public passages and places, or for the purpose of providing a site for erecting any gasometer, cistern, or other apparatus as aforesaid, and for otherwise improving the said borough and town, or tithing or hamlet respectively, for the absolute purchase of all such buildings, erections, doors, cellars, steps, projections, encroachments, lands, tenements, or hereditaments, or any of them, or for the damage to be done thereto respectively in the execution or for the purposes of this Act, and to take down or alter all or any of such buildings, erections, steps, projections, encroachments, tenements, and hereditaments, so to be purchased, or any part or parts of the same respectively, and also to appropriate all or any part of the lands, tenements or hereditaments so to be purchased for all or any of the purposes aforesaid, as they the said Commissioners respectively shall think fit: Provided always that if the said Commissioners shall not within the space of five years, to be computed from the passing of this Act, agree for or cause to be valued and paid for as hereinafter mentioned, the several buildings, lands, tenements and hereditaments, which they are hereby empowered to purchase as aforesaid, or so much thereof as they shall deem necessary or proper for the purposes of this Act, then and from thenceforth the powers and authorities hereby granted to them for such purpose shall cease determine and be utterly void: Provided also, that the quantity of land to be purchased for the purpose of providing a site for erecting such gasometer, cistern or other apparatus as aforesaid, shall not exceed two statute acres in the whole.

89. And be it further Enacted, That it shall be lawful for all bodies politic corporate or collegiate, and all corporations, whether aggregate or sole, and all feoffees in trust, executors, administrators, husbands, guardians, committees of or for lunatics and idiots, and other trustees whomsoever, not only for and on behalf of themselves and their heirs and successors, but also for and on behalf of their respective *cestui que* trusts, whether infants or issue unborn, lunatics idiots or femes covert, and also to and for all femes covert who are or shall be seized in their own right, and to and for all persons, whether tenants for life or tenants in tail, general or special, or for years determinable on any life or lives, and to and for all and every person or persons whomsoever who are or shall be seized possessed of or interested in any lands, houses, erections, cellars, steps, projections, encroachments, lands, tenements or other hereditaments, or any part thereof, which the said Commissioners are by this Act

enabled to purchase for any of the purposes of this Act, to treat contract and agree with the said Commissioners for their respective jurisdictions, for the sale thereof, or any part thereof, and to sell and convey all or any part thereof, and all the estate, right, title and interest whatsoever of in and to the same, to the said Commissioners respectively and their successors for any of the purposes of this Act; and all contracts, agreements, bargains, sales and conveyances, which shall be made by virtue and in pursuance of this Act, shall, without any fine or fines, recovery or recoveries, or other conveyances or assurances in the law whatsoever, be good valid and effectual, to all intents and purposes, not only to convey all estate, right, interest, use, property, claim and demand whatsoever of the said several and respective *cestui que* trusts, but all claiming or to claim by from or under them, any law, statute, usage or any other matter or thing whatsoever to the contrary thereof notwithstanding; and all bodies politic corporate or collegiate, corporations aggregate or sole, and all feoffees in trust, executors, administrators, husbands, guardians, committees, trustees, and all other persons, whomsoever, are and shall be hereby indemnified for what they shall do by virtue and in pursuance of this Act.

90. And be it further Enacted, That if any body politic corporate or collegiate, or any corporation, whether aggregate or sole, or any feme covert, or any tenant for life, or any tenant in tail, general or special, or for years determinable on any life or lives, owner or owners, occupier or occupiers, or other person or persons whomsoever, interested in any building or buildings, erection or erections, projecting in or upon any of the carriageways or footways within the said borough and town, tithing or hamlet respectively, or

of any door or doors, cellar or cellars, or any steps
belonging thereto, or in any other projection or encroachment upon any such carriageway or footway
whatsoever, or in any lands, houses or other buildings,
tenements or hereditaments, which the said Commissioners respectively are enabled by this Act to purchase or treat for, shall refuse to treat, contract or
agree as aforesaid, or by reason of absence or otherwise shall be prevented from treating, contracting
or agreeing, or shall decline or refuse to sell, convey
and dispose of the premises whereof or wherein or
whereunto they respectively shall be so seised, possessed, interested or entitled as aforesaid, or their
respective rights, titles, claims or interest, into or
upon the same, or any part thereof, unto the said
Commissioners respectively, or to such person or
persons as they shall nominate for the purposes, and
according to the tenor, true intent and meaning of
this Act, or shall not or cannot produce or make out
a clear title to the premises they are in the possession
of, or to the interest they claim therein, to the satisfaction of the said Commissioners respectively, or if
any dispute or difference shall arise touching such
purchase or purchases, then and in every such case
the said Commissioners respectively are hereby empowered and authorized, before any general or quarter
sessions of the peace to be holden for the said
borough and town, if the matter cause or thing happen or arise within the said borough or town, or if
the matter cause or thing happen or arise within the
said tithing or hamlet of *Speenhamland*, before any
general or quarter sessions to be holden for the said
county of *Berks*, or any adjournment of such general
or quarter sessions respectively, to give or cause to
be given to such owner or owners, or the principal
officer or officers of such bodies politic, corporate,
or collegiate, or to leave or cause to be left at the

I

house of the tenant in possession, ten days notice in writing, denoting, and particularly describing the lands, buildings, houses, tenements, or other hereditaments intended to be purchased, and purporting that the value thereof shall be adjusted and settled by a jury at the said respective sessions or adjournment thereof; and the Justices at the said sessions respectively, or any adjournment thereof, upon proof to them, made of such notice having been given or left, are hereby authorized and required to charge the grand jury at such sessions assembled, or the jury to try prisoners at such sessions, well and truly upon their oaths to assess the value of the said lands, buildings, houses, tenements or other hereditaments comprised in the notices so given, and the damages and recompense to be awarded or given for the same to the respective owner or owners thereof according to their respective interests therein, and to which said jury the said Commissioners respectively, and all persons interested in the said lands, buildings, houses, tenements or other hereditaments, shall have their lawful challenges; and the jury being so sworn and charged as aforesaid, and after proper evidence on oath to them given concerning the nature, quality or value of the lands, houses, buildings, tenements, or other hereditaments so to be sold or conveyed as aforesaid, shall, by their verdict, assess the damages and recompense to be given for the same to the respective owner or owners, occupier or occupiers thereof, according to their respective interests therein, and such verdict of the said jury, and the judgment of the said Justices upon the same, shall be final binding and conclusive to the said Commissioners respectively, and to all person and persons interested in the said lands, buildings, houses, tenements and other hereditaments; and such verdict, and the judgment of the Justices thereupon, shall be fairly entered and kept among the records of the sessions. for the said county, town or place respectively, and the same or true copies thereof shall be taken to be good and effectual evidence and proof in any court of law or equity whatsoever, and all persons may have recourse to the same gratis, and take copies thereof, paying eightpence for every seventy-two words, and so in proportion for any greater or less number of words: Provided always, that in case the sum or sums so assessed by the said jury, and ordered and adjudged to be paid by the said Commissioners respectively, as a satisfaction to the owners, occupiers and others for their respective interests in the said premises, shall not be paid, tendered, left or deposited according to the true intent and meaning of this Act, within three calendar months after the same shall have been so assessed, ordered and adjudged, then and in such case the verdict of the said jury shall not be binding upon the said parties, any thing herein contained to the contrary thereof in anywise notwithstanding.

91. And be it further Enacted, That in every case where a verdict shall be given by any such jury for more money than shall have been previously offered by or on behalf of the said Commissioners respectively, as a price recompense or satisfaction for any such buildings, lands, tenements or hereditaments as aforesaid, or for any estate right or interest therein, all the costs and expenses to be incurred in summoning impannelling and returning such jury, taking such inquisition, and the attendance of witnesses and recording the verdict of judgment thereon, shall be borne by the said Commissioners respectively out of the monies to be raised by virtue of this Act for their respective jurisdictions, and in case such costs and expenses shall not be paid to the party or person

entitled to receive the same within fourteen days after the time appointed for payment thereof, then the same shall and may be levied and recovered by distress and sale of any goods and chattels vested in the said Commissioners respectively, or their treasurer or treasurers (unless the treasurer or treasurers of the said Commissioners respectively shall pay such costs and expenses out of any monies received by him by virtue of this Act, which he is hereby authorized to do,) under a warrant to be issued for that purpose by any Justice of the peace for the said county town or place respectively, which warrant any such Justice is hereby authorized and required to issue under his hand and seal on application made to him for the purpose by the party or person entitled to receive such costs and expenses; and in every case where a verdict shall be given by any such jury for no more or for less money than shall have been previously offered by or on the behalf of the said Commissioners respectively, as such price recompense or satisfaction as aforesaid, all the costs and expenses to be incurred as aforesaid shall be borne by the party or parties refusing or neglecting to treat and agree as before mentioned, or with whom the said Commissioners respectively shall have had any disagreement or dispute concerning such price recompense or satisfaction as aforesaid; but in all cases where any person or persons, party or parties shall have been prevented by absence from entering into any treaty with the said Commissioners respectively, the costs and expenses so incurred shall be borne by the said Commissioners respectively, in manner aforesaid; and in all cases where any difference shall arise touching the amount of such costs and expenses, the same shall be settled and ascertained by any Justice of the peace for the said county town or place respectively, not interested in the matter in question, who is hereby authorized and required to examine into and settle the same at a time and place to be by him appointed, after summoning the parties interested therein to attend him for that purpose, and to appoint a time and place for payment thereof; and where the costs shall be payable by the party or parties having had such disagreement or dispute with the said Commissioners respectively as aforesaid, the amount thereof having been first paid by the said Commissioners respectively, may be deducted by them out of the monies awarded to be paid to such party or parties as so much money advanced for his, her or their use, and the payment or tender of the balance of such money shall be deemed and taken to all intents and purposes whatsoever to be a payment or tender of the whole money awarded and adjudged to such party or parties; or otherwise, if such costs and charges be not paid upon demand after being so ascertained as aforesaid, the same may be recovered by the said Commissioners respectively, from the party or parties liable to the payment thereof, by action of debt or on the case in any of His Majesty's courts of record, together with full costs of suit.

92. Provided always, and be it further Enacted, That nothing herein contained shall authorize or empower the said Commissioners, or any person or persons acting by or under their authority, to take, use, injure or damage, for the purposes of this Act, any house or other building, garden, orchard, yard, park, paddock, planted walk or avenue to a house, or any inclosed ground planted and set apart as a nursery for trees, without the consent in writing of the owners or occupiers thereof, and persons interested therein respectively, other than and except those specified in the Schedule annexed to this Act.

93. Provided always, and be it further Enacted, That if any of the messuages, buildings, lands, tenements or hereditaments mentioned and described in the Schedule hereunto annexed, or any of the owners thereof, or of the persons in whose possession or occupation the same or any part thereof are or is stated or described to be, or any person or persons otherwise interested therein, shall happen by mistake to be misnamed or incorrectly described, such misnomer or incorrect description shall not prevent or retard the execution of this Act, but the same premises, and every part thereof, shall and may be purchased, sold, assessed and valued in manner as in this Act mentioned, and afterwards conveyed, disposed of and applied for, and to the purposes of this Act, as fully and effectually as if the same was or were properly named and described in the said Schedule hereunto annexed; provided it shall appear to any two Justices of the peace for the county town or place wherein such messuages, buildings, lands, tenements or hereditaments shall be situate, and be certified by writing under their hands, that such omission, misnomer or inaccurate description proceeded from mistake, or that the real owners or occupiers of such messuages, buildings, lands, tenements or hereditaments had notice that the same respectively would be wanted for the purposes of this Act.

94. And be it further Enacted, That all sales conveyances and assurances of any lands, tenements or hereditaments to be made to the said Commissioners respectively, shall be in the form or to the effect following; (that is to say,)

"I,   of   in consideration of the sum of
" to me paid by the Commissioners for the

" improvement of the borough and town of *Newbury,.*
" [*or,* of the tithing or hamlet of *Speenhamland,* in
" the county of *Berks, as the case may be,*]acting
" by virtue of an Act of Parliament made in the
" sixth year of the reign of King GEORGE the
" Fourth, intituled, [*here set forth the title of this*
" *Act,*] Do hereby grant and convey to the said
" Commissioners and their successors, All [*here*
" *describe the premises to be conveyed,*] and all my
" right, title and interest in and to the same, and
" every part thereof; to hold to the said Commis-
" sioners and their successors for ever. In witness
" whereof, I have hereto set my hand and seal
" this   day of   in the year of our
" Lord   ."

And every such sale, conveyance and assurance
so made shall be good valid and effectual to all intents
and purposes whatsoever, any law, statute, usage or
custom to the contrary notwithstanding.

95. And be it further Enacted, That every sum
of money to be agreed for or awarded or assessed
as aforesaid, shall within three calendar months after
the same shall have been so agreed for awarded or
assessed, be paid out of the monies to be received
by virtue of this Act ; and upon payment or tender
thereof to the party or persons respectively entitled
to such monies, or their agents, or depositing the
same in the Bank of England (as the case may be)
in manner by this Act directed and required, all the
estate, right, title, interest, use, trust, property, claim,
and demand, in law and equity, of the person or persons respectively to whose credit or use the same
shall have been paid, into and out of such lands,
buildings, houses, tenements or hereditaments, shall
vest in the said Commissioners for their respective

jurisdictions in trust for effecting the purposes of this Act, and they shall be deemed in law to be in the actual seisin and possession thereof to all intents and purposes whatsoever, as fully and effectually as if every person having any estate in the premises had actually conveyed the same by lease and release, bargain and sale enrolled, feoffment with livery of seisin, fine, common recovery, surrender, or any other conveyance or assurance whatsoever: and such payments shall not only bar all right, title, interest, claim and demand of the person or persons to whose use or credit such payments shall have been made as aforesaid, but also extend to and be deemed and construed to bar the dower of the wife and wives of such person and persons, and all estates tail and other estates in possession, reversion, remainder or expectancy, and the issue of such person and persons claiming under them, as effectually as fines or common recoveries would do if levied or suffered by the proper parties in due form of law.

96. And be it further Enacted, That if any money shall be paid or agreed or awarded to be paid for the purchase of any lands, tenements or hereditaments, purchased taken or used by virtue of this Act for the purposes thereof, which shall belong to any body politic, corporate or collegiate, or to any feoffee in trust, executor, administrator, husband, guardian, committee or other trustee for or on behalf of any infant, lunatic, idiot, feme covert, or other *cestui que* trust, or to any person whose lands tenements or other hereditaments are limited in strict or other settlement, or to any person under any other disability or incapacity whatsoever, such money shall, in case the same shall be equal to or exceed the sum of two hundred pounds, with all convenient speed be paid into the Bank of England, in the name and with

privity of the Accountant General of the Court of
Exchequer, to be placed to his account there *ex parte*
the Commissioners for executing this Act, according
to their respective jurisdictions, pursuant to the
method prescribed by an Act, passed in the first year
of the reign of His present Majesty King GEORGE
the Fourth, intituled, " An Act for the better securing
" Monies and Effects paid into the Court of Exche-
" quer at Westminster on account of the Suitors of
" the said Court, and for the appointment of an
" Accountant General and Two Masters of the said
" Court, and for other purposes," and the general
orders of the said court, and without fee or reward :
and shall when so paid in be applied, under the direction and with the approbation of the said court, to be
signified by an order made upon a petition, to be
preferred in a summary way by the person or persons
who would have been entitled to the rents and profits
of the said lands tenements and hereditaments, in the
purchase or redemption of the land-tax, or discharge
of any debt or debts, or such other incumbrances, or
part thereof, as the said court shall authorize to be
paid affecting the same lands tenements or hereditaments, or affecting other lands tenements or hereditaments standing settled therewith to the same or the
like uses intents or purposes ; or where such money
shall not be so applied, then the same shall be laid out
and invested, under the like direction and approbation
of the said court, in the purchase of other lands
tenements or hereditaments, which shall be conveyed
and settled to for and upon such and the like uses,
trusts, intents and purposes, and in the same manner
as the lands tenements or hereditaments which shall
be so purchased taken or used as aforesaid stood
settled or limited, or such of them as at the time of
making such conveyance and settlement shall be
existing undetermined and capable of taking effect;

and in the meantime and until such purchase shall be made, the said money shall by order of the said court, upon application thereto, be invested by the said Accountant General in his name in the purchase of three pounds per centum consolidated, or three pounds per centum reduced bank annuities ; and in the meantime and until the said bank annuities shall be ordered by the said court to be sold for the purposes aforesaid, the dividends and annual produce of the said consolidated or reduced bank annuities shall from time to time be paid, by order of the said court, to the person or persons who would for the time being have been entitled to the rents and profits of the said lands tenements and hereditaments, so hereby directed to be purchased, in case such purchase or settlement were made.

97. And be it further Enacted, That if any money so agreed or awarded to be paid for any lands tenements or hereditaments to be purchased taken or used for the purposes aforesaid, and belonging to any corporation, or to any person or persons under any disability or incapacity as aforesaid, shall be less than the sum of two hundred pounds, and shall amount to or exceed the sum of twenty pounds, then and in all such cases the same shall, at the option of the person or persons for the time being entitled to the rents and profits of the lands tenements or hereditaments so purchased taken or used, or of his her or their guardian or guardians, committee or committees, in case of infancy idiotcy or lunacy, to be signified in writing under their respective hands, be paid in the Bank of England, in the name and with the privity of the said Accountant General of the Court of Exchequer, and be placed to his account as aforesaid, in order to be applied in manner hereinbefore directed ; or otherwise the same shall be paid, at the like option, to two

trustees, to be nominated by the person or persons making such option, and approved of by three or more of the said Commissioners for their respective jurisdictions for executing this Act, (such nomination and approbation to be signified in writing under the hands of the nominating and approving parties,) in order that such principal money and the dividends arising thereon may be applied in manner hereinbefore directed, so far as the case may be applicable, without obtaining or being required to obtain the direction or approbation of the Court of Exchequer.

98. And be it further Enacted, That where such money so agreed or awarded to be paid as last before mentioned shall be less than twenty pounds, then and in all such cases the same shall be applied to the use of the person or persons who would for the time being have been entitled to the rents and profits of the lands tenements or hereditaments so purchased taken or used for the purposes of this Act, in such manner as the said Commissioners respectively shall think fit; or in case of infancy idiotcy or lunacy, then such money shall be paid to his her or their guardian or guardians, committee or committees, to and for the use and benefit of such person or persons so entitled respectively.

99. And be it further Enacted, That in case the person or persons to whom any sum or sums of money shall be awarded for the purchase of any lands tenements or hereditaments to be purchased by virtue of this Act shall refuse to accept the same, or shall not be able to make a good title to the premises to the satisfaction of the said Commissioners respectively, or in case such person or persons to whom such sum or sums of money shall be awarded as aforesaid cannot

be found, or if the person or persons entitled to such lauds tenements and hereditaments be not known or discovered, then and in every such case it shall be lawful for the said Commissioners respectively, or any three or more of them, to order the said sum or sums of money so awarded as aforesaid to be paid in the Bank of England, in the name and with the privity of the Accountant General of the Court of Exchequer, to be placed to his account to the credit of the parties interested in the said lands tenements or hereditaments [*describing them,*] subject to the order control and disposition of the said Court of Exchequer; which said Court of Exchequer, on the application of any person or persons making claim to such sum or sums of money, or any part thereof, by motion or petition, shall be and is hereby empowered in a summary way of proceeding, or otherwise, as to the same court shall seem meet, to order the same to be laid out and invested in the public funds, and to order distribution thereof, or payment of the dividends thereof, according to the respective estate or estates, title or interest of the person or persons making claim thereunto, and to make such other order in the premises as to the said court shall seem just and reasonable; and the cashier or cashiers of the Bank of England, who shall receive such sum or sums of money, is and are hereby required to give a receipt or receipts for such sum or sums of money, mentioning and specifying for what and for whose use the same is or are received for such person or persons as shall pay any such sum or sums of money into the Bank as aforesaid.

100. Provided always, and be it further Enacted, That when any question shall arise touching the title of any person to any money to be paid into the Bank of England in the name and with the privity of the Accountant General of the Court of Exchequer in

pursuance of this Act, for the purchase of any lands, tenements or hereditaments, or of any estate right or interest in any lands tenements or hereditaments, to be purchased in pursuance of this Act, or to any bank annuities to be purchased with any such money, or the dividends or interest of any such bank annuities, the person or persons who shall have been in possession of such lands tenements or hereditaments at the time of such purchase, and all persons claiming under such person or persons, or under the possession of such person or persons, shall be deemed and taken to have been lawfully entitled to such lands tenements or hereditaments according to such possession, until the contrary shall be shown to the satisfaction of the said Court of Exchequer, and the dividends and interest of the bank annuities to be purchased with such money, and also the capital of such bank annuities, shall be paid applied and disposed of accordingly, unless it shall be made appear to the said court that such possession was a wrongful possession, and that some other person or persons was or were lawfully entitled to such lands tenements or hereditaments, or to some estate or interest therein.

101. And be it further Enacted, That where by reason of disability or incapacity of the person or persons or corporation entitled to any lands tenements or hereditaments to be purchased under the authority of this Act, the purchase money for the same shall be required to be paid into the Court of Exchequer, and to be applied in the purchase of other lands tenements and hereditaments to be settled to the like uses in pursuance of this Act, it shall be lawful for the said Court of Exchequer to order the expenses of all purchases to be from time to time made in pursuance of this Act, or so much of such expenses as the court shall deem reasonable, to be paid by the said Com-

missioners for their respective jurisdictions out of the monies to be received by virtue of this Act, who shall from time to time pay such sums of money for such purposes as the said court shall direct.

102. And be it further Enacted, That all and every person and persons, body and bodies politic corporate and collegiate, in possession of any houses or buildings, lands tenements or hereditaments, which shall be purchased by and vested in the said Commissioners respectively by virtue of this Act, or of any part thereof, shall at the end of six calendar months next after notice shall be given to him her or them for that purpose under the hands of five or more of the said Commissioners respectively, peaceably and quietly deliver up the possession of the said premises to such person or persons as shall be authorized by the said Commissioners respectively to take possession thereof, they the said Commissioners respectively making such satisfaction to every such person or persons, bodies politic corporate or collegiate, in case he she or they shall be required to quit before the expiration of his her or their term in the premises, as the said Commissioners respectively shall deem just and reasonable; and in case any dispute or difference shall arise touching or concerning the same, such satisfaction or compensation shall be settled and ascertained by a jury in manner hereinbefore mentioned ; and in case any such person, or body politic corporate or collegiate, shall refuse to give up such possession as aforesaid, it shall be lawful for the said Commissioners respectively to issue their precept or warrant, signed by any three or more of the said Commissioners respectively, to the sergeants at mace of and for the said borough and town of *Newbury*, or the constable bailiff or tithingman of the said tithing or hamlet of *Speenhamland*, (as the case may require,)

to deliver possession of the premises to such person or persons as shall in such precept or warrant be nominated to receive the same, and the said sergeants, constable, bailiff or tithingman respectively, are hereby required to deliver such possession accordingly, and to levy such costs as shall accrue upon the issuing or execution of such precept or warrant on the person or persons so refusing to give possession as aforesaid, by distress and sale of his her and their goods, returning the overplus (if any) to the owner thereof on demand.

103. AND whereas by reason of the purchases which the said Commissioners for their respective jurisdictions are hereby empowered to make, they may happen to be possessed of some building or buildings, piece or pieces of ground over and above what may be necessary for effecting the improvements hereby directed to be made, or for other the purposes of this Act; BE it further Enacted, That it shall be lawful for the said Commissioners respectively to sell and dispose of such building or buildings, piece or pieces of ground, either together or in parcels, as they shall find most advantageous and convenient, to such person or persons as shall be willing to contract for and purchase the same; and the money to arise by sale of such building or buildings, piece or pieces of ground, shall be applied to the respective purposes of this Act, but the purchaser or purchasers thereof shall not be answerable or accountable for the misapplication or nonapplication thereof.

104. Provided always, and be it further Enacted, That the said Commissioners for their respective jurisdictions, before they shall sell and dispose of any such buildings or grounds, shall first offer the same for sale to the person or persons respectively from

whom they shall have purchased such buildings or grounds, and in case such person or persons shall not then and thereupon agree or shall refuse to repurchase the same, then and in every such case an affidavit, to be made and sworn before a Master Extraordinary in the High Court of Chancery, or before one or more of His Majesty's Justices of the peace for the county town or place, by some person or persons noway interested in the said buildings or grounds, stating that such offer was made by or on behalf of the said Commissioners respectively, and that such offer was not then and thereupon agreed to, or was refused by the person or persons to whom the same was so offered, shall in all courts whatsoever, be sufficient evidence and proof that such offer was made and was not agreed. to, or was refused by the person or persons to whom it was made (as the case may be;) but in case such former owner or owners shall be desirous of repurchasing the same, and cannot agree with the said Commissioners respectively in regard to the price to be paid for the purchase thereof, then and in such case the price or value thereof shall be settled and ascertained by a jury in like manner as the price or value of any hereditaments to be purchased or taken by the said Commissioners respectively for the purposes of this Act is hereinbefore directed to be settled and ascertained, and the costs and charges of ascertaining and determining the same shall be borne and paid in like manner as hereinbefore is directed (with respect to purchases made by the said Commissioners respectively, *mutatis mutandis*; and all monies to arise by any sales which may be made by the said Commissioners respectively of the said premises, or any part or parts thereof, shall be applied to the purposes of this Act, but the purchasers thereof having paid his her or their purchase monies to the treasurer or treasurers of the said Commissioners respectively, and obtained his or their receipt or receipts for the same, shall not be liable to see to the application of the said monies, or answerable or accountable for the mis-application or nonapplication of the same.

105. And be it further Enacted, That it shall be lawful for the said Commissioners respectively to enter into any contract or contracts for lighting, watching, paving, flagging, widening, cleansing, watering, improving, extending and regulating the several markets, squares, streets, ways, lanes, public passages and places within the said borough and town, or tithing or hamlet respectively, or any of them, or for furnishing materials or other matters or necessary things whatsoever, or for any other the purposes of this Act; but before any such contract or contracts shall be entered into, fourteen days notice at least shall be given in some public newspaper circulated in the said county of *Berks,* and such other public notice as the said Commissioners respectively shall for that purpose order or direct, expressing the purpose or purposes of such contract or contracts, in order that any person or persons willing to undertake the same may make proposals for that purpose, to be offered to the said Commissioners respectively at a certain time and place in such notice to be mentioned, and the said Commissioners respectively shall and they are hereby required to take security from any such contractors for the due performance of his or her contract.

106. And be it further Enacted, That it shall be lawful for the said Commissioners respectively from time to time, and at all times hereafter, to compound and agree with any person or persons on account of any breach or nonperformance of such contract or contracts for such sum or sums of money,

K 3

or upon such terms and conditions, as they the said Commissioners respectively shall think proper.

107. And be it further Enacted, That every such contract or contracts shall specify the several works to be done, and the prices to be received or paid for the same, and the time or times when the said works are to be completed, and the penalties to be suffered in case of nonperformance thereof, and shall be signed by the said Commissioners respectively, or any three or more of them, and also by the person or persons contracting to perform such work respectively, which contract or contracts shall be entered in a book or books to be kept for that purpose by the clerk to the said Commissioners respectively.

108. Provided always, and be it further Enacted, That no contract which shall be made by the said Commissioners respectively for any of the purposes of this Act shall be binding upon the said Commissioners respectively as individuals or in their private capacity, nor shall any of the said Commissioners respectively personally, or their respective estates, be answerable for or subject to the payment of any of the mortgages or annuities to be granted in pursuance of this Act; and all money which shall be expended by or recovered against any of the said Commissioners respectively, or any person or persons employed by them, by means of any action, prosecution or appeal to be brought by or against them or any of them touching the execution of this Act, shall be borne and defrayed out of the money which shall come to the hands of the treasurer to the said Commissioners respectively, or any other person by virtue of this Act; provided nevertheless, that nothing herein contained shall extend to exonerate or discharge any of the said Commissioners, their houses,

lands, tenements, hereditaments, goods, chattels or effects from the payment of the rates or assessments to be raised by virtue of this Act.

109. And be it further Enacted, That if any person or persons shall at any time or times hereafter obstruct, hinder or molest any collector or collectors, surveyor or surveyors, or other officer or officers, or any workmen or other person or persons whomsoever, who shall be employed by virtue of this Act, or in any manner concerned in the execution thereof, in the performance or execution of his or their duty or work, every person so offending shall for every such offence forfeit and pay any sum not exceeding five pounds.

110. And be it further Enacted, That all offences whatsoever which by virtue or under the authority of this Act, are or shall be subject to or punishable with any pecuniary penalties, fines or forfeitures, for the recovery of which no express provision is hereinbefore made, shall and may in every case be heard, adjudged and determined by or before any Justice or Justices of the peace in and for the county town or place wherein the offence shall be committed, in a summary way, upon information or complaint made and exhibited in writing, (and which shall in every case be made and exhibited within three calendar months at furthest, next after the committing of such offences respectively, and not afterwards ;) and upon such information or complaint as aforesaid, the said Justice or Justices shall examine into the matter thereof, and if upon the confession of the party or parties accused, or on the oath of any one or more credible witness or witnesses, the party or parties accused shall be convicted of having committed such offence or offences, then and in every such case the

penalty or penalties, fine or fines, forfeiture or forfeitures hereby made payable in respect of such
offence or offences, together with the costs of conviction, to be ascertained by such Justice or Justices,
shall be forthwith paid by the party or parties so
convicted as aforesaid; and in case such party or
parties so convicted shall refuse or neglect to pay the
same forthwith, then, except in cases otherwise
provided by this Act, the same shall and may by
warrant or warrants under the hand and seal or hands
and seals of any Justice or Justices, (which he and
they is and are hereby empowered and required to
grant,) be levied and recovered, together with full
costs of conviction and recovery thereof, to be ascertained by such Justice or Justices, by distress and
sale of the goods and chattels of such offender or
offenders, rendering the overplus of the money arising
by such sale (if any) to the party or parties whose
goods and chattels shall be distrained, one moiety of
which penalties, not herein directed to be otherwise
applied, shall be paid to the informer, and the other
moiety shall be paid to the overseers of the poor of
the parish wherein the offence shall have been committed and applied toward the relief of the poor
thereof; and it shall be lawful for the said Justice
or Justices to order the offender or offenders so convicted to be detained in safe custody, until return can
be conveniently made to such warrant or warrants of
distress, unless the said offender or offenders shall
give sufficient security, to the satisfaction of such
Justice or Justices, for his, her or their appearance
before the said Justice or Justices on such day or
days as shall be appointed for the return of such
warrant or warrants of distress, such day or days not
being more than ten days from the time of taking any
such security, and which security the said Justice or
Justices is and are hereby empowered to take by way

of recognizance or otherwise; but if upon the return of such warrant or warrants it shall appear that no sufficient distress can be had whereupon to levy the said penalty or penalties, fine or fines, forfeiture or forfeitures, and such costs as aforesaid, and the same shall not be forthwith paid, or in case it shall appear to the satisfaction of such Justice, either by the confession of the offender or offenders or otherwise, that the offender or offenders hath or have not sufficient goods and chattels whereon such penalties, forfeitures, fines, costs, and charges may be levied were a warrant of distress issued, such Justice shall not be required to issue such warrant of distress, and thereupon it shall be lawful for the said Justice or Justices, and he and they is and are hereby required and empowered by warrant or warrants under his hand and seal or their hands and seals, to commit such offender or offenders to the gaol for the county, town or place wherein the offence shall be committed, thereto remain without bail or mainprize for any term not exceeding three calendar months, or until such offender or offenders shall have fully paid such penalty or penalties, fine or fines, forfeiture or forfeitures, and all costs attending such proceedings as aforesaid, to be ascertained by such Justice or Justices, or shall otherwise be discharged by due course of law.

111. And be it further Enacted, That all and every Justice and Justices before whom any person or persons shall be convicted of any offence against this Act, shall and may cause such conviction to be drawn up in the form or to the effect following; (that is to say,)

" BE it Remembered, that on the   day
" of   in the year of our Lord   ,   is

"convicted before   of His Majesty's
"Justices of the peace for the   of having
"[*here state the offence;*] and I [*or*, we] the said
"Justice [*or*, Justices] do adjudge him, her or them
"to forfeit and pay the sum of   Given under
"my hand and seal [*or*, our hands and seals] the day
"and year aforesaid."

112. And be it further Enacted, That where any distress shall be made for any sum or sums of money to be levied by virtue of this Act, the distress itself shall not be deemed unlawful, nor the party or parties making the same be deemed a trespasser or trespassers, on account of any defect or want of form in the information, summons, conviction, warrant of distress or other proceeding relating thereto, nor shall the party or parties distraining be deemed trespasser or trespassers on account of any irregularity that shall be afterwards done by the party or parties distraining, but the person or persons aggrieved by such irregularities may recover satisfaction for the special damage in an action on the case.

113. And be it further Enacted, That if any person or persons shall think himself, herself or themselves aggrieved by any rate or assessment which shall be made or demanded in pursuance of this Act, or by any bye-law or any other order, judgment or determination of the said Commissioners for their respective jurisdictions, or by any penalty imposed, or by any conviction made, or by any other thing done in pursuance of this Act, (save and except in such cases where any other judgment or determination is herein directed to be final and conclusive, and save and except in such cases for which any particular method of relief is herein appointed,) such person or persons may appeal to the Justices of the peace

at the general quarter sessions of the peace, to be holden for the County of *Berks* next after the cause of complaint shall have arisen, or at any adjournment of such sessions, the person or persons appealing first giving or causing to be given to the person or persons appealed against, or to the clerk to the said Commissioners respectively, in case such appeal shall be made against any rate or assessment, bye-law, rule, order; judgment or determination, matter or thing made or done by the said Commissioners respectively, fourteen days notice in writing of his, her and their intention to bring such appeal, and the cause and matter thereof, and within six days next after such notice entering into a recognizance before some Justice of the peace for the said county, with two sufficient sureties, conditioned to try such appeal, and abide the order of and to pay such costs as shall be awarded by the Justices at such sessions or adjournment thereof; and the Justices at such sessions, upon due proof of such notice having been given, and of such recognizance having been entered into as aforesaid, shall hear and finally determine every such appeal in a summary way, and award such costs to the party appealing or appealed against as the said Justices shall think proper, and shall and may at their discretion discharge or mitigate any fine penalty or forfeiture, and may order any money, to be returned which shall be levied in pursuance of any such bye-law, rule, order, judgment or determination of the said Commissioners respectively, and may also order and award such further satisfaction to be made to the party injured as they the said Justices shall think reasonable, and the determination of the said Justices, in their said general quarter sessions, or adjournment thereof, shall be final binding, and conclusive to all intents and purposes whatsoever.

114. Provided always, and be it further Enacted, That on any appeal from any rate or assessment to be made for the purposes of this Act, the Justices of the sessions where such appeal shall be heard shall and mny amend the same in such manner as may be necessary for giving relief, without quashing or altering such rates or assessments with respect to the other persons mentioned in the same; but if upon appeal from the whole rate or assessment it shall be found necessary to set aside the same, then and in such cases the said Justices shall and may order a new rate or assessment to be made in the manner herein directed.

115. And be it further Enacted, That no person shall in any action prosecution or other proceeding whatsoever relating to or concerning the execution of this Act, be deemed an incompetent witness on account of his or her being charged with or liable to pay any rate or assessment to be raised levied and collected by virtue of this Act.

116. And be it further Enacted, That the said Commissioners respectively may sue and be sued in the name of their clerk for the time being, and all actions and suits which may be necessary or expedient to be brought for the recovery of any penalty or sum or sums of money due or payable by virtue of this Act, or for or in respect of any other matter or thing relating to this Act, may be brought in the name of the said clerk: and no action or suit which may be brought, commenced or prosecuted by or against the said Commissioners respectively, or any of them, by virtue or on account of this Act in the name of their clerk, shall abate or be discontinued by the death, suspension or removal of such clerk, or by any act or default of such clerk done or suffered, without the consent or direction of the said Commissioners respectively, but the clerk to the said Commissioners respectively for the time being shall be always deemed plaintiff or defendant in every such action or suit (as the case may be,) except in such action or actions as shall be prosecuted between the said Commissioners respectively and their clerk for the time being, in which action or suit any one of the said Commissioners respectively shall or may be plaintiff or defendant, (as the case may be): Provided always, that every such clerk or Commissioner in whose name any action or suit shall be commenced prosecuted or defended in pursuance of this Act, shall always be reimbursed and paid out of the monies to be raised by virtue of this Act, all such damages, costs, charges and expenses as such clerk or Commissioner shall be put to or become chargeable with by reason of his being so made plaintiff or defendant therein, and no such clerk or Commissioner shall be personally answerable or liable for the payment of the same, or any part of the same, unless such action or suit shall arise in consequence of his own wilful neglect or default, or have been brought or commenced without the order or direction of the said Commissioners respectively, or any five or more of them.

117. And be it further Enacted, That in all cases where any costs, charges, damages, compensations or expenses are by this Act directed to be paid or received by the said Commissioners respectively, to or from any body corporate or politic, Commissioners trustees or other person or persons, and the amount of such costs, charges, damages, compensations or expenses shall not be agreed on by or between the said parties, and is not herein or hereby otherwise directed or authorized to be ascertained and recovered, the

L

same shall be settled and determined by any two or more Justices of the peace of the county town or place wherein the matter in difference shall arise, who are hereby authorized and required within seven days next after complaint or application shall be made to them for that purpose by the party aggrieved or entitled to claim compensation, to enquire into, and upon the oath or affirmation of one or more credible witness or witnesses ascertain and determine, the same in a summary way; and in case the amount of such costs, charges, damages, compensations and expenses, so to be ascertained and determined as aforesaid, shall not be paid and discharged within ten days after the same shall have been so ascertained and determined, and demand of payment having been duly made, the amount thereof or of so much thereof as shall then remain unpaid, together with any penalties which may then have been incurred in consequence of such nonpayment, shall and may upon proof by the oath or affirmation of one or more credible witness or witnessess of such demand and neglect of payment, be levied and recovered by distress and sale of the goods and chattels of the party or parties to whom it shall belong to pay the same, together with the costs of such distress and sale, by warrant under the hands and seals of two or more Justices of the peace for the said county town or place, which warrant they are accordingly hereby authorized and directed to grant; and the amount which shall be recovered and received under such warrant shall be paid to the party or parties authorized to claim and receive the same under the provisions herein contained, who after deducting the necessary charge of making such distress and sale, shall pay over the surplus thereof (if any) to the party or parties so refusing or neglecting, or the amount may be recovered in any of His Majesty's courts at Westminster, by action of debt, wherein no essoin, protection or wager of law, nor more than one imparlance, shall be allowed.

118. And be it further Enacted, That when and as often as any sum or sums of money shall be directed or ordered to be paid by any Justice or Justices of the peace in pursuance of this Act, as or by way of compensation or satisfaction for any materials or costs, or for any damage spoil or injury of any nature or kind whatsoever done or committed by the said Commissioners, or any person or persons acting by or under their authority, and such sum or sums of money shall not be paid by the said Commissioners to the party or parties entitled to receive the same within ten days after demand in writing shall have been made from the said Commissioners, in pursuance of the direction or order made by such Justice or Justices, and in which demand the order of such Justice or Justices shall be stated, then and in such case the amount of such compensation or satisfaction shall and may be levied and recovered by distress and sale of the goods and chattels vested in the said Commissioners by virtue of this Act, or of the goods and chattels of their treasurer for the time being, under a warrant to be issued for that purpose by such Justice or Justices, which warrant any such Justice or Justices is and are hereby authorized and required to grant under his hand and seal, or their hands and seals, on application made to him or them for that purpose by the party or parties entitled to receive such sum or sums of money, as or by way of compensation or satisfaction for any such materials, costs, damages, spoil or injury as aforesaid ; and in case any overplus shall remain after payment of such sum or sums of money and the costs and expenses of hearing and determining the matter in dispute, and also the

costs and expenses of such distress and sale, then and in such case such overplus shall be returned, on demand, to the said Commissioners or to their treasurer for the time being, as the case may be: Provided always, that it shall be lawful for such treasurer to retain, out of any monies which he shall have received or shall receive in pursuance of this Act, all such damages, costs, charges and expenses as he shall have sustained or be put unto by virtue of any such warrant as aforesaid.

119.   And be it further Enacted, That no plaintiff or plaintiffs shall recover in any action to be commenced against any person or persons for any thing done in pursuance of this Act, unless notice in writing shall have been given to the defendant or defendants twenty-eight days before such action shall be commenced of such intended action, signed by the attorney of the plaintiff or plaintiffs, specifying the cause of such action, nor shall the plaintiff or plaintiffs recover in any such action if tender of sufficient amends shall have been made to him her or them, or to his her or their attorney by or on behalf of the defendant or defendants before such action brought; and in case no such tender shall be made, it shall be lawful for the defendant or defendants in any such action, by leave of the court, at any time before issue joined to pay into court, such sum of money as he she or they shall think proper, whereupon such proceeding order and judgment shall be made and given in and by such court as in other actions where the defendant is allowed to pay money into court.

120.   And be it further Enacted, That no action or suit shall be brought against any person or persons for any thing done in pursuance of this Act, or in relation to the matters herein contained, after three

calendar months from the fact committed, and every such action or suit shall be brought and tried in the county where the cause of action shall have arisen, and not elsewhere; and the defendant and defendants in every such action or suit shall or may, at his or their election, plead specially, or the general issue, and give this Act and the special matter in evidence at any trial, and that the same was done in pursuance and under the authority of this Act. and if the same shall appear to have been so done, or if such action or suit shall have been brought before the expiration of twenty-eight days after such notice shall have been given as aforesaid, or after sufficient satisfaction made or tendered as aforesaid, or after the time limited for bringing the same, or shall be brought in any other county or place than as aforesaid, then and in every of the cases aforesaid the jury shall find a verdict for the defendant or defendants, and upon such verdict, or if the plaintiff or plaintiffs shall be nonsuited, or discontinue his her or their action or suit after the defendant or defendants shall have appeared, or if upon any demurrer, judgment shall be given against the plaintiff or plaintiffs, then and in every such case the defendant or defendants shall recover treble costs, and have such remedy for recovering the same as any other defendant or defendants hath or have in other cases by law.

121. And be it further Enacted, That it shall be lawful for the said Commissioners respectfully, from time to time to direct any prosecution or prosecutions at the assizes or quarter sessions for the county of *Berks,* or for the said borough and town, if the offence be cognizable within the said borough and town, for any public nuisance whatsoever which shall be committed or suffered or permitted within the said borough and town, or tithing or hamlet respec-

tively, and to direct and order the expenses of such prosecution or prosecutions to be paid and borne by and out of the respective funds to be raised and provided for the purposes of this Act.

122. And be it further Enacted, That no order rate or assessment, judgment or other proceeding made, touching or concerning any of the matters aforesaid, or touching or concerning the conviction of any offender or offenders against this Act, shall be quashed or vacated for want of form only, or be removed or removable by writ of *certiorari*, or any other writ or process whatsoever, in any of His Majesty's courts of record at Westminster; any law, statute or usage to the contrary thereof in anywise notwithstanding.

123. And be it further Enacted, That it shall be lawful for the said Commissioners respectively to reward any informer or informers as they shall think proper, so as such reward shall not exceed the amount of the penalty or forfeiture proved by the information of such informer or informers to have been incurred; any thing herein contained to the contrary notwithstanding.

124. And be it further Enacted, That all orders or notices which are directed or required to be given by this Act, or which are or may be directed and required to be given by any rules, orders or bye-laws made or to be made in pursuance of this Act, or which shall or may be necessary for carrying into execution any of the powers of the same, or any such rules, orders or bye-laws made or to be made in pursuance of this Act, or which shall or may be necessary for carrying into execution any of the powers of the same, of which the manner of serving

the same is not particularly directed by this Act, the service of any such order or notice, either on the person to whom the same ought to be given, or leaving the same or a true copy thereof, signed by the clerk for the time being to the said Commissioners respectively, at the dwelling-house or usual or last place of abode of such person, shall be good and sufficient service of any such order or notice.

125. And be it further Enacted, That in all cases wherein it may be requisite to serve any notice or notices upon the said Commissioners respectively, or any writ or writs or other legal proceedings, the service thereof upon the clerk or clerks of the said Commissioners respectively, or at the office of such clerk or clerks, or left at his or their last or usual place of abode, or at the office of the said Commissioners respectively, or upon any one of the said Commissioners, or left at his last or usual place of abode, or upon any agent or other officer employed by the said Commissioners respectively, or left at his last or usual place of abode, shall be deemed good and sufficient service of the same respectively on the said Commissioners respectively.

126. Provided always, and be it further Enacted, That nothing in this Act contained shall extend or be construed to extend in any way to change, lessen, abridge, impeach, annul prejudice or destroy any rights, privileges, jurisdictions, immunities, rents, tolls, stallage, dues, duties and customs belonging, due, or anywise appertaining to, or which at the time of the passing of this Act are received by the Mayor Aldermen and Burgesses, either as lords of the manor or reputed manor of *Newbury* aforesaid, or as lords or owners of the said borough and

town, or of the fairs and markets within the same, or in or by any other right title or capacity whatsoever, or of the Mayor for the time being of the said borough and town as clerk of the markets therein, or in any other lawful capacity; but all and every such rights, privileges, jurisdictions, immunities, rents, tolls, stallage, dues, duties and customs may be exercised, demanded, exacted, received and enjoyed in as full and ample a manner to all intents and purposes as the same are enjoyed, or as the Mayor Aldermen and Burgesses are entitled to enjoy at the passing of this Act.

127. And be it further Enacted, That nothing in this Act contained shall extend or be construed or deemed or taken to extend to affect, extinguish, defeat, abridge, impeach, annul, prejudice or destroy the right title or interest of the Reverend Doctor *Thomas Penrose*, Lord of the Manor of *Speenhamland*, or the Lord of the Manor for the time being, of in or to the seigniories, rights, royalties, franchises, jurisdictions, rents, services, liberties, privileges, powers and authorities appendant, appurtenant, incident or belonging to the said manor of *Speenhamland*, ; but the said Reverend Doctor *Thomas Penrose*, Lord of the said Manor, and the Lord of the said Manor for the time being, shall have, hold, use, exercise, take and enjoy all and every the seigniories, rights, royalties, franchises, pre-eminences, jurisdictions, rents, services, powers, authorities, liberties, privileges, advantages and emoluments whatsoever, to the said manor belonging, or incident, appendant, appurtenant and now or heretofore usually exercised holden or enjoyed therewith; and the said Reverend Doctor *Thomas Penrose*, or the Lord of the said Manor of *Speenhamland*, for the time being, shall and may demand exercise, exact, take and enjoy all such

rents, customs, dues, duties, services, privileges,
rights, immunities, profits and advantages, with all
powers and remedies for enforcing the same in such
and the like manner, and as fully and beneficially to
all intents and purposes, as if this Act had not been
passed; any thing herein contained to the contrary
thereof in anywise notwithstanding.

128. And be it further Enacted, That if any person or persons shall advance and pay any money in
discharge of the expenses of applying for and obtaining this Act, such person or persons, shall be
repaid the same with interest after the rate of five
pounds per centum per annum, out of the monies
which shall be first raised to defray the expenses of
this Act.

129. And be it further Enacted, That the costs
charges and expenses preparatory to and attending
the passing and obtaining this Act, shall be borne and
defrayed by the owners of the lands, tenements,
houses, factories, shops, warehouses, coachhouses,
yards, gardens, cellars, vaults, and other buildings
and hereditaments within the said borough and town
and parish of *Newbury,* and tithing or hamlet of
Speenhamland respectively, for which purpose the said
Commissioners respectively shall levy one or more
separate rate or rates, assessment or assessments, upon
such owners respectively; and such rate or rates,
assessment or assessments, shall in the first instance
be paid by the respective tenants or occupiers of such
lands, tenements, houses, factories, shops, warehouses,
coach-houses, yards, gardens, stables, cellars, vaults,
and other buildings and hereditaments, who shall and
may and they are hereby empowered to deduct the
same from the first rent which shall become due from

them to such owners respectively next after payment of such rate or rates, assessment or assessments.

130.   Provided always, and be it further Enacted, That this Act or any thing herein contained shall not extend or be construed to extend to release or discharge the trustees or commissioners named or appointed under or by virtue of any Act or Acts of Parliament for repairing any highway road or turnpike road, within or passing through the limits of this Act, or any part thereof, from the expenses of widening amending or repairing any of the streets, roads, lanes, entries, or other public passages and places of and within the said limits, but the said trustees and commissioners shall be subject and remain liable to the expenses of widening amending and repairing the same, and every of them, in the same manner and to the same extent as they were before the passing of this Act, and as they would have been if this Act had not passed.

131.   And be it further Enacted, That this Act shall be deemed and taken to be a Public Act; and shall be judicially taken notice of as such, by all Judges Justices and others, without being specially pleaded.

Schedule to which this Act refers.

Description of Property.	Owners.	Occupiers.
CHEAP STREET.		
House and shop —	Anthony Morris —	Himself.
Ditto —	John Gater Marriner —	William Rowles.
Ditto —	Thomas Smith —	Grace King;
Ditto —	Richard Patey —	John Armstrong
Ditto —	Ann Smith —	William Palmer.
Ditto —	Sarah White —	Thomas Samuels.
Ditto —	John Martin —	Benjamin Garland.
Ditto —	Ann Smith —	Edward Griffin.
Ditto —	Ditto —	William Crosswell.
Ditto —	Weavers Company —	William Walter.
Ditto —	Churchwardens of Thatcham —	John Britton.

Description of Property.	Owners.	Occupiers.
BRIDGE STREET.		
Part of a house	Thomas Stockwell Saxon	Messrs. Slocock and Co.
Ditto	Proctor of Saint Mary's Hill Alms-houses in Newbury, and the Representatives of Osmon Vincent.	George Vincent.
Garden Ground, called the Island	Churchwardens of Newbury	Mrs. Wilmott.
BARTHOLOMEW STREET.		
Part of court or yard, called the Litten	Corporation of Newbury, as Trustees of Saint Bartholomew Hospital in Newbury	Elizabeth Best.
Outhouse	Ditto	Ditto.
Part of farm yard	Ditto	Richard Compton.
The London Apprentice public-house, yard, garden, and stable	Charles Alderman	John Cotton.
Part of the cheese fair close	George Wright	George Liddiard.
	The Corporation of Newbury, as Trustees of Saint Bartholomew's Hospital in Newbury	John Palmer.
House	John Trumplett	William Darling.

House and Offices —	The Devisees of Daniel Fossick —	William Somerset.
Ditto —	Ditto —	Ann Jones.
Ditto —	Ditto —	William Hanson.

NEW LINE OF ROAD FROM THE TOP OF BARTHOLOMEW STREET, LEADING TOWARDS NEWTOWN.

Part of East Field —	Heir or devisee of Thomas Townsend —	John Cotten and others.
Ditto —	The Corporation of Newbury, as Trustees of Saint Bartholomew's Hospital in Newbury —	Richard Compton.
Ditto —	James Ebenezer Bicheno —	William Purdue.
Ditto —	The Corporation of Newbury, as Trustees of Saint Bartholomew's Hospital in Newbury —	Late Edward Smith
Ditto —	Heir or devisee of Thomas Burton —	Thomas Smith.
Ditto —	William Budd —	George Liddiard.
Ditto —	The Trustees of the Presbyterian Meeting House in Newbury —	Henry Butler.
Ditto —	The Corporation of Newbury, as Trustees of Saint Bartholomew Hospital in Newbury —	Richard Compton.
Part of a meadow —	Heir or devisee of Sarah Baily —	Benjamin Grobetty.

M

Description of Property.	Owners.	Occupiers.

NEW STREET FROM BARTHOLOMEW STREET TO THE MARKETPLACE.

Description of Property.	Owners.	Occupiers.
Half Moon public house, and offices	Edmund Slocock	Thomas Gore.
Stables, pigsties and yard	Ditto	Ditto.
House and outbuildings	Mary Pearce	Edward Stroud.
The Catherine Wheel public house, stables, yard and outhouses	Thomas Smith	John Knight.

NEW STREET FROM BARTHOLOMEW STREET TO THE TITHING OF GREENHAM.

Description of Property.	Owners.	Occupiers.
Black Boys public house, yard, garden, stables and out-buildings	Churchwardens of Newbury	William Dredge.
Tenement, outbuildings and garden	Ann Lovegrove	Herself.
Ditto	Ditto	Sarah Hill.
Ditto	Ditto	Benjamin Lovegrove.
Dwelling-house, outbuildings, yard and garden	Manasseh James	William Dredge.
Meadow	Heir or devisee of Thomas Gleed	Hannah Harrison.
Part of East Field	Corporation of Newbury	William Purdue.
Ditto	Heir or devisee of Thomas Townsend	Late Edward Smith.

Description	Owner / Devisee	Occupier
Part of East Field	Corporation of Newbury —	Richard Compton.
Ditto —	Heir or devisee of Thomas Burton	Thomas Smith.
Ditto —	William Budd —	Himself.
Ditto —	Heir or devisee of Thomas Burton	Thomas Smith.
Ditto —	Corporation of Newbury —	
Ditto —	The Corporation of Newbury, as Trustees of Saint Bartholomew's Hospital in Newbury	Richard Compton.
Ditto —	Churchwardens of Newbury —	Daniel Challis.
Ditto —	James Bicheno —	James Legge.
Ditto —	Heir or devisee of Thomas Townsend	James Legge.
Ditto —	James Bicheno —	James Legge.
Tenement, outhouses, yard and garden	Corporation of Newbury —	Thomas Moss.
A plot of garden ground —	Miss Dobson —	Mrs. Collett.
Ditto —	John Gater Marriner —	William Baggs.
Two plots of garden ground	Frederick Page, Esquire —	William Liddiard.

MARKETPLACE.

Description	Owner / Devisee	Occupier
House and shop —	Thomas Stockwell Saxon —	Himself.
Ditto —	Richard Perry —	
Ditto —	James Sims —	Richard Knight.
Ditto —	Charles Trip —	John Trumplett.
House —	Thomas Bance —	Unoccupied.
Stable, offices and warehouses	Corporation of Newbury —	Christopher Hunter & others
Part of workhouse garden	Ditto —	Churchwardens and Overseers of Newbury.

M 2

Description of Property.	Owners.	Occupiers.
House, yard, malthouse, gardens and outhouses	Richard Compton	John Packer.
House, yard and outhouses	Sarah Bennett	Thomas Record.
Garden	—	John Trumplett.
The old Town Hall, gaol, and butchers market.	Corporation of Newbury	
Victualling house	Ditto	Richard Perry.
The new town-house	Ditto	

SPEENHAMLAND.

Description of Property.	Owners.	Occupiers.
House and Shop	William Jaques	Himself.
Ditto	Ditto	James Kitcat.
House	John Grist and Elizabeth his wife	Unoccupied.
Part of meadow and yard	John Padbury	Himself and John Henry Padbury.
Cottage and outhouses	The devisees of Thomas Ward Blagrave deceased	James James.
Ditto	Ditto	William Self.
Ditto	Ditto	John Williams.
House	Ditto	Unoccupied.
Ditto	Thomas Poor	Himself.
Corner of house	Charles Alderman	Edmund E. W. Gale.

A
TRANSLATION

OF THE

Charter of Incorporation

OF THE

BOROUGH OF NEWBURY,

IN THE

COUNTY OF BERKS.

Anno 38 *Eliz.* *A.D.* 1596.

———

By W. ILLINGWORTH, Esq.

Deputy Keeper of the Records at the Tower of London.

GRANT for the MAYOR
ALDERMEN and BUR-
GESSES of the Borough of
NEWBERY.

THE QUEEN to all to whom &c. Greeting
WHEREAS our Borough of NEWBERY in our
County of Berks is an ancient and populous Borough
and the Burgesses and Inhabitants within the Borough aforesaid from time whereof the memory of
man is not to the contrary have had used and enjoyed
divers Liberties Franchises Immunities and Pre-eminences as well by our Charter as by the Charters of
many of our Progenitors and Predecessors Kings of
England heretofore made and granted to them and
to their Successors as by reason of divers prescrip-
tions and customs in the same Borough from of old
time used   AND WHEREAS our beloved Subjects the Inhabitants of the same Borough have very
humbly besought us that WE would for our part
shew and extend our royal grace and munificence to
the said Inhabitants of the same Borough AND
that for the better rule government and improvement
of the same Borough WE would vouchsafe by these
our Letters Patent to ratify confirm approve make
reduce and newly to create the said Inhabitants of
the same Borough into one body corporate and politic
WE therefore being WILLING that hereafter for
ever there shall be continually observed in the

same Borough one certain and indubitable mode of
and for the keeping of the Peace and the rule and
government of the people there AND that the
Borough aforesaid may hereafter for ever be and
remain a Borough of Peace and Quiet to the dread
and terror of the bad and for the reward of the good
AND that our Peace and other the Acts of Justice
there shall be kept without further delay AND
HOPING that if the said inhabitants of the same
Borough and their Successors shall be able from
our Grant to enjoy more ample liberties and privileges than that they may conceive themselves espe-
cially and more firmly bound to perform and exhibit
[all] the service in their power to us our Heirs and
Successors OF our especial grace and of our certain
knowledge and mere motion HAVE WILLED,
ORDAINED, CONSTITUTED and GRANT-
ED and by these presents for us our Heirs and
Successors DO WILL ORDAIN CONSTITUTE
DECLARE and GRANT that the said Borough of
Newbery in the said County of Berks may and shall be
for the future a free Borough of itself And that the
Burgesses and Inhabitants of that Borough and their
Successors may and shall be hereafter for ever by force
of these presents one Body Corporate and Politic in
Deed Fact and Name by the name of the Mayor
Aldermen and Burgesses of the Borough of Newbery
AND them by the name of the Mayor Alder-
men and Burgesses of the Borough of Newbery
WE do by these presents for us our Heirs and Suc-
cessors erect make ordain constitute confirm and
declare as one Body Corporate and Politic in Deed
Fact and Name really and to the full AND that by
the same name they shall have perpetual succession
AND that they by the name of the Mayor Aldermen
and Burgesses of the Borough of Newbery may and
shall hereafter for ever be persons able and capable

in law to have purchase receive and possess Lands
Tenements Liberties Privileges Jurisdictions Franchises and Hereditaments of whatsoever kind nature
or species they shall be to them and their Successors
in fee and perpetuity and also Goods and Chattels
and other things whatsoever of whatsoever kind
nature or species they shall be AND also to give
grant demise and assign Lands Tenements and Hereditaments And to do and execute all and singular
other acts and things by the name aforesaid AND
that by the same name of the Mayor Aldermen and
Burgesses of the Borough of Newbery aforesaid
they shall and may be able to plead and be impleaded
answer and be answered unto defend and be defended
in whatsoever Courts and Places and before whatsoever the Judges and Justices and other the Officers
and Ministers of us our Heirs and Successors in all
Suits Plaints Causes Matters and Demands whatsoever of whatsoever kind nature or species they
may be and in the same manner and form as others
our liege Subjects within our kingdom of England
[being] persons able and capable in law may and
shall be able to plead and be impleaded answer
and be answered unto defend and be defended
and to have purchase receive possess give grant
and demise AND that the aforesaid Mayor
Aldermen and Burgesses of the said Borough
of Newbery and their Successors shall have for
ever a Common Seal to serve for the transacting
of their Causes and Businesses whatsoever and those
of their Successors AND THAT it may and shall be
lawful for the same Mayor Aldermen and Burgesses
and their Successors from time to time at their pleasure, to break change and to make anew such Seal as
to them shall seem best to be done AND FUR-
THER WE WILL and by these presents for us our
Heirs and Successors do ORDAIN and GRANT to

the Mayor Aldermen and Burgesses of the Borough
of Newbery aforesaid that henceforth there may and
shall be within the Borough aforesaid from time to
time thirty one of the most honest Burgesses of the
Borough aforesaid (of whom the Mayor and Aldermen
there for the time being WE will to be seven) who shall
be called and named the Capital Burgesses and
Counsellors of the same Borough Which said thirty
one Capital Burgesses and Counsellors shall make
shall be and at all times hereafter for ever shall be
called the Common Council of the Borough aforesaid
for all things matters causes and businesses touching
or concerning the Borough aforesaid and the good
rule state and government of the same Borough AND
that all the aforesaid Capital Burgesses not being in
the Office of Mayor and Aldermen of the Borough
aforesaid be and shall be assisting and aiding to the
Mayor and Aldermen of the Borough aforesaid for
the time being in the transacting of all Causes and
Matters touching or concerning the same Borough
AND FURTHER WE WILL and by these presents
for us our Heirs and Successors of our especial grace
and certain knowledge and mere motion DO GRANT
to the aforesaid Mayor Aldermen and Burgesses of
the Borough of Newbery aforesaid and to their
Successors for ever that they and their Successors by
the Mayor of the Borough aforesaid for the time being
and the Aldermen and Capital Burgesses being the
Common Council of such Borough for the time being
or by the major part of the same Mayor Aldermen
and Capital Burgesses (of whom the Mayor of the
same Borough for the time being and three Aldermen
of the same Borough and twelve Capital Burgesses
of the Common Council of the same Borough WE will
to be sixteen) may and shall have the full power and
authority of framing constituting ordaining and
making from time to time such reasonable Statutes

and ordinances whatsoever which to them according
to their sound discretion shall seem good wholesome
useful honest and necessary for the good rule and
government of the Burgesses Artificers and Inhabitants of the Borough aforesaid for the time being
AND for the declaring in what manner and order the
aforesaid Mayor Aldermen and Burgesses and the
Artificers Inhabitants and Residants ot the said Borough shall behave and conduct and demean themselves in their Office Ministries and Businesses
within that Borough and the Limits thereof for the time
being and otherwise for the further good common
weal and government of such Borough and the Victualling of the same Borough and also for the better
preservation government disposition letting and
demising of the Lands Tenements Possessions Re-
venues and Hereditaments given granted or assigned
or hereafter to be given and granted to the aforesaid
Mayor Aldermen and Burgesses and their Successors
and of other the matters and causes whatsoever
touching or in anywise concerning the Borough aforesaid or the estate right and interest of the same
Borough AND that they and their Successors by
the Mayor for the time being and the Aldermen and
Capital Burgesses being the Common Council of
the same Borough or by the major part of them as
aforesaid as often as they shall have framed made
ordained or established such Laws Statutes and
Ordinances in form aforesaid may impose and assess
such and the like reasonable pains penalties and
punishments by imprisonment of the body or by
fines and amerciaments or by either of them against
and upon all Persons offending against such laws
statutes and ordinances or any one or more of them
as and which to the same Mayor Aldermen and Burgesses and the Common Council of the Borough
aforesaid for the time being or the major part of them

as aforesaid shall seem to be reasonable and requisite
AND the same Fines and Amerciaments they may
and shall have power to levy and have without the
impediment of us our heirs and Successors ALL and
singular which laws statutes and ordinances so to
be made as aforesaid We will to be observed under
the pains in the same to be contained NEVER-
THELESS so that such laws statutes ordinances
imprisonments fines and amerciaments be not
repugnant or contrary to the laws statutes customs
or rights of our Kingdom of England AND
for the better execution of the same our will
and Grants in this behalf WE have AS-
SIGNED NOMINATED CONSTITUTED and
MADE And by these presents for us our Heirs and
Successors do ASSIGN NOMINATE CON-
STITUTE and MAKE our beloved Bartholomew
Yate the now Mayor of the Borough aforesaid to be
the first and modern Mayor of the Borough aforesaid
WILLING that the same Bartholomew Yate shall be
and continue in the Office of Mayor of the same
Borough from the making of these presents, until the
feast of Saint Matthew the Apostle next ensuing and
from the same feast until another Burgess of the said
Borough shall be constituted and sworn to that
Office according to the ordinances and constitutions
in these presents expressed and declared if the same
Bartholomew Yate shall so long live ALSO WE
have ASSIGNED NOMINATED and CONSTI-
TUTED And by these presents for us our Heirs and
Successors do ASSIGN NOMINATE CONSTI-
TUTE and MAKE our beloved Edward Holmes
Roger Saunderson Henry Coxe Gabriel Cox John
Kystle and William Bakesdaile Burgesses of the
Borough aforesaid to be the six first and modern
Aldermen of the Borough aforesaid to be continued
in the same Office until the feast of Saint Matthew

the Apostle next ensuing and from the same feast
during the natural lives of the same Edward Holmes
Roger Saunderson Henry Coxe Gabriel Cox John
Kystle and William Backsdale unless in the mean
time for the misrule and government or for any other
reasonable cause they or any of them shall be removed
from their Offices of Alderman of the Borough
aforesaid ALSO WE have ASSIGNED NOMI-
NATED CONSTITUTED and MADE and by
these presents for us our Heirs and Successors do
ASSIGN NOMINATE CONSTITUTE and
MAKE our beloved Christopher Walker William
Chamber Thomas Goddard Richard Chefe, John
Hunt Gabriel Cox the younger Thomas Getnet
Christopher Grant Simon Johnson John Greenways
Robert Cooke Thomas Bate Thomas Newman
William Rippon Richard Yonge Thomas Parker,
Richard Gardner Henry Yate John Shipton Maurice
Shipton Henry Shipton Christopher Twiste John
Backesdale and Thomas Backesdale to be the first
and modern Capital Burgesses of the Borough
aforesaid to be continued in the same Office during
their lives Unless in the mean time for their mis-
governance in that behalf they shall be removed from
that Office AND FURTHER WE WILL and by
these presents for us our Heirs and Successors DO
GRANT to the aforesaid Mayor Aldermen and Burgesses of the Borough of Newbery aforesaid and their
Successors that the aforesaid Capital Burgesses
[being] the Common Council of the Borough aforesaid
or the major part of them from time to time hereafter
for ever may and shall have the power and authority
yearly and every year on the feast of Saint Matthew
the Apostle to assemble themselves or the major part
of them in the Guildhall of the Borough aforesaid
and there to continue until they or the major part
of them there then assembled shall elect or nominate

N

one Mayor from amongst themselves for the year
following to be elected and named in form following
AND that they shall and may have power before
they shall depart thence there to nominate and elect
one of the aforesaid Capital Burgesses who shall be
the Mayor of the Borough aforesaid for one whole
year then next following And that he after he shall
so as aforesaid be elected and nominated as Mayor
of the said Borough before he be admitted to execute
that Office shall take his Corporal oath upon the Holy
Evangelists of God yearly on Monday next after the
said feast of Saint Matthew the Apostle before the
last Mayor his Predecessor or in his absence before
the Aldermen of the Borough aforesaid or two of
them in the presence of such of the aforesaid Capital
Burgesses of the Common Council of the said Borough for the time being and of other the Burgesses
of the Borough aforesaid who shall then be present
in the Guildhall of the said Borough rightly well and
faithfully to execute that office in all things touching
such Office AND that after such Oath so taken he
shall take upon himself the Office of Mayor of the
Borough aforesaid for one whole year then next
following AND further he ought shall and may have
power to execute [such Office] until another of the
aforesaid Capital Burgesses of the Borough aforesaid shall in due form be elected constituted and
sworn as Mayor of the said borough And that the
aforesaid Aldermen above named and their successors hereafter to be elected and nominated before
they shall be admitted to such Office of Aldermen of
the borough aforesaid shall take a Corporal Oath
before the Mayor and the rest of the Capital Burgesses of the said borough for the time being or the
major part of them rightly well and faithfully to
execute such Office of Alderman in all things touching that Office AND MOREOVER WE WILL

and by these presents for us our Heirs and Successors DO GRANT to the aforesaid Mayor Aldermen and Burgesses of the borough aforesaid and to their Successors that if it shall happen that the Mayor of the borough aforesaid at any time hereafter within one year after he shall be constituted and sworn to the Office of the Mayoralty of the said borough as aforesaid or any one of the Aldermen of the borough aforesaid above named shall die or be removed from his Office (which said Aldermen and every of them not behaving themselves well in that Office we will to be removable at the pleasure of the Mayor of the borough aforesaid and of the major part of the Capital Burgesses aforesaid for the time being) that then and so often it may and shall be lawful for the said Capital Burgesses the Common Council of the borough aforesaid for the time being or the major part of them to elect and nominate one other honest and fit person out of the said Capital Burgesses of the borough aforesaid as and for the Mayor of the borough aforesaid into the place of him so dead or removed from his Office in a convenient time after he shall so die or be removed from his Office and [to elect and nominate] one out of the aforesaid Capital Burgesses who before that time was the elder [and] senior of the aforesaid borough into the place of the same Alderman so dead or removed from his Office within fifteen days after the aforesaid Alderman shall so die or be removed from his Office AND if any one or more of the rest of the aforesaid thirty-one Capital Burgesses of the borough aforesaid shall die or be removed from his or their Office (whom and every of them not behaving themselves well in their Office we will to be removable at the pleasure of the Mayor of the borough aforesaid and of the major part of the aforesaid Capital Burgesses aforesaid for the time being) then that such of the rest of the

aforesaid Capital Burgesses being the Common
Council of the borough aforesaid who shall be assembled in the Guildhall of the borough aforesaid or the
major part of them so assembled on the feast of Saint
Matthew the Apostle may and shall have power to
elect and constitute one or as many as shall be deficient of the aforesaid number of thirty-one the best
and most honest of the Burgesses of the borough
aforesaid into the place of the same Capital Burgess
or Capital Burgesses so dead or removed from his or
their Offices AND that he or they so elected and
constituted shall have and exercise such Office to
which he or they shall be so elected so long as they
shall behave themselves well in such Office AND
that the aforesaid Mayor so newly elected before he
shall execute such Office of the Mayoralty shall take
a Corporal Oath before the Aldermen aforesaid or
two of them and of such of the aforesaid thirty-one
Capital Burgesses of the borough aforesaid who shall
be then present And that the Alderman and Aldermen so newly elected before they shall execute such
Office shall likewise take a Corporal Oath before the
Mayor of the borough aforesaid and the Common
Council of the same or the major part of them and
this when and as often as the case shall so happen
AND FURTHER WE WILL and by these presents for us our Heirs and Successors DO GRANT
to the aforesaid Mayor Aldermen and Burgesses of
the borough aforesaid and their Successors that they
and their Successors may have in the borough aforesaid one eminent and discreet Man in form hereinafter expressed to be elected and nominated who
shall be and be named the High Steward of the
borough aforesaid AND WE WILL that the aforesaid High Steward of the borough aforesaid for the
time being shall have and appoint from time to time
at his pleasure [by his writing] signed with his proper

hand and sealed with his seal one or more Men
learned in the law to be the Deputy of the said
Steward AND we have assigned constituted and
made and by these presents for us our Heirs and
Successors do assign nominate ordain constitute
and make our beloved Counsellor John Woolley
Knight our Secretary for the Latin language to be
the first and modern High Steward of the borough
aforesaid so to be continued in the same Office during
the natural life of the said John Woolley Knight
AND that after the death of the same John Woolley
Knight the Mayor Aldermen and Capital Burgesses
for the time being or the major part of them shall
and may have power on the said feast of Saint Matthew the Apostle to elect nominate and constitute
one eminent and discreet Man from time to time as
High Steward of the borough aforesaid AND that
he who shall be elected constituted and nominated
High Steward of the said Borough as aforesaid after
the death of the said John Woolley Knight may and
shall have exercise and enjoy such Office of High
Steward by himself or his sufficient Deputy in form
aforesaid to be appointed for one whole year then next
following and afterwards until another High Steward of
the Borough aforesaid shall be elected and constituted
to that Office AND FURTHER WE WILL and by
these presents for us our Heirs and Successors DO
GRANT to the aforesaid Mayor Aldermen and Burgesses of the Borough of Newbery aforesaid and their
Successors that hereafter for ever they may have and
that there may and shall be in the Borough aforesaid
two Officers who shall be and be called the Serjeants at
the Mace for the executing of the processes mandates
and other businesses pertaining to the Office of Serjeants
at the Mace in the Borough from time to time to be
executed and performed Which said Serjeants at the
Mace shall be appointed nominated and elected by

the aforesaid Mayor Aldermen and Common Council
of the borough aforesaid or by the major part of them
yearly on the feast of Saint Matthew the Apostle and
they and every of them shall be attendant from time to
time upon the Mayor of the borough aforesaid for the
time being AND that the aforesaid two Serjeants at
the Mace so to be elected and nominated may and
shall be sworn before the Mayor Aldermen and
Common Council of the borough aforesaid or the
major part of them for the time being (of whom the
Mayor for the time being we will to be one) well and
faithfully to execute such Offices and that after such
Oath so taken they ought shall and may execute
such Office for one whole year then next following so
long as they shall behave themselves well AND
FURTHER WE WILL and ORDAIN and by
these presents for us our Heirs and Successors DO
GRANT to the aforesaid Mayor Aldermen and Burgesses of the borough aforesaid and to their Successors for ever that the aforesaid Serjeants at Mace to
be appointed in the borough aforesaid shall carry and
bear before the Mayor of the borough aforesaid for
the time being every-where within the said borough of
Newbery the Suburbs Liberties and Precincts of the
same golden or silver Maces and engraven and orna-
mented with the sign of the Arms of the Kingdom of
England AND we have assigned constituted and
ordained And by these presents for us our Heirs and
Successors do assign nominate constitute and make
our beloved Subjects Giles Hynde and Thomas
Bullock Burgesses of the borough aforesaid to be the
first and modern Serjeants at the Mace of the borough
aforesaid to be continued in the same Offices until
the feast of Saint Matthew the Apostle next following
and from the same day until two other Inhabitants of
the same borough shall in due form be elected and
sworn to the Offices of Serjeants at the Mace accord-

ing to the form in these our Letters Patent mentioned
AND WE WILL And by these presents for us our
Heirs and Successors DO GRANT to the aforesaid
Mayor Aldermen and Burgesses of the borough
aforesaid and to their Successors that they and their
Successors hereafter for ever may have and hold and
shall and may be able to have and hold in the Guildhall of the same borough one Court of Record on
every Tuesday in every week throughout the year to
be holden before the mayor of the borough aforesaid
for the time being and in the absence of the said
Mayor before one of the Aldermen of the borough
aforesaid for the time being deputed by the same
Mayor for the time being AND that in such Court
they may hold by plaints to be levied in the same
Court all and all manner of pleas actions suits and
demands of whatsoever trespasses with force and arms
or otherwise done or to be made in contempt of us our
Heirs and Successors and of all and all manner of
pleas upon the case debt account covenant deceit
detinue of charters deeds muniments and taking of
chattels and detaining of Cattle and Chattels and
other Contracts from whatsoever causes or things
arising or happening within the borough aforesaid and
the limits and precincts thereof so that the debts and
accounts or damages in the said actions suits pleas
and plaints exceed not the sum of twenty marks AND
that as often as any person or persons whosoever
would implead any other person or persons whomsoever possessing or holding Lands Tenements Rents
or Hereditaments within the borough aforesaid the
Limits and Precincts of the same concerning the same
Lands Tenements Rents and Hereditaments so often
he or they so wishing to implead may prosecute our
writ of Right Patent out of our Court of Chancery of
England to be directed to the said Mayor of the
borough aforesaid upon which said Writ in the Court

aforesaid before the Mayor of the said borough for the time being or his Deputy he or they so as aforesaid wishing to implead shall make his protestation to prosecute his plaint upon the aforesaid Writ made in the nature of a Writ of Assize of Novel Disseisin Mortancestor attaint or in the nature of any other Action or Writ whatsoever at the Common Law in manner as the matter or case demands and requires AND that such pleas plaints and actions as well real as personal and mixed shall be there heard and determined before the Mayor of the borough aforesaid for the time being or in his absence before one of the Aldermen of the same borough deputed by the Mayor of the borough aforesaid for the time being in the Guildhall of the borough aforesaid by such and the like processes and forms according to the law and custom of the Kingdom of England whereby and in manner as shall be consonant to our law and in as ample a manner and form and as is used and accustomed or can or ought to be done in any other Court of Record in any other borough or Corporate town within this Kingdom of England AND WE WILL and for us our Heirs and Successors by these presents do GRANT and ORDAIN that the Serjeants at Mace of the Borough aforesaid for the time being or any of them shall make and execute within the borough aforesaid and the Liberties thereof all Juries Panels Inquisitions Attachments Precepts Mandates Warrants Judgments Processes and other things whatsoever necessary to be done in the Causes aforesaid or other Causes whatsoever touching or concerning the said borough as to them shall seem meet according to the exigency of the law or according to the custom of the borough aforesaid and in manner as in like cases is used and ought to be done in any other Court of Record in any other borough or Corporate town within this

Kingdom of England AND WE WILL and by
these presents for us our Heirs and Successors do
GRANT to the aforesaid Mayor Aldermen and Burgesses of the borough of Newbery aforesaid and
their Successors that there may and shall be hereafter
for ever within the borough aforesaid four honest and
discreet Men learned in the laws of this kingdom of
England and not more who shall be and be called
Attornies of the Court aforesaid and shall plead and
transact all causes actions and plaints whatsoever
between whatsoever Persons as well Plaintiffs and
Demandants as Defendants and Tenants concerning
any Lands Tenements Debts Demands and other
things and matters whatsoever determinable in the
same Court AND MOREOVER WE WILL
ORDAIN and GRANT for us our Heirs and Successors to the aforesaid Mayor Aldermen and Burgesses of the Borough of Newbery aforesaid and
their Successors that whensoever it shall happen that
any of the Attornies aforesaid at any time hereafter
shall die or be removed from their Office (which said
Attornies and every of them misbehaving themselves
in their Offices WE will to be removable at the pleasure of the aforesaid Mayor and of the major part of
the aforesaid Capital Burgesses the Common Council
of the borough aforesaid for the time being) that then
and so often it may and shall be lawful for the aforesaid Mayor and the major part of the Capital Burgesses of the Borough aforesaid in a convenient time
to elect and nominate one other sufficient person in
the place of such Attorney so dead or removed from
his Office WHICH said Attorney so as aforesaid
elected and nominated shall and may have power
to execute and exercise the Office of Attorney aforesaid during his natural life unless in the mean time he
shall be removed from his aforesaid Office for mal-
practice therein so as aforesaid AND thus when and

so often as the case shall so happen AND FUR-
THER WE have granted And by these presents
for us our Heirs and Successors DO GRANT to the
aforesaid Mayor Aldermen and Burgesses of the
borough of Newbery aforesaid and to their Successors
that they and their Successors hereafter for ever may
and shall have the return of all and all manner and
singular Writs Precepts Bills Processes and Warrants
for us our Heirs and Successors as well of Assizes of
Novel Disseisin and other Assizes and Writs of Right
Patent and of all and all manner of other our Writs
Bills Precepts Processes and Warrants to be executed
and returned within the borough aforesaid AND
FURTHER WE do WILL and GRANT for us our
Heirs and Successors to the aforesaid Mayor Aldermen and Burgesses of the borough aforesaid and to
their Successors for ever that they may have hold and
keep and may and shall be able to have hold and keep
in the borough aforesaid yearly for ever four Fairs or
Marts yearly to be holden every year for ever the first
of the said four Fairs commencing on the day of the
Annunciation of our Lord and to continue through all
that day and the second Fair or Mart of the said four
Fairs or Marts commencing on the day of the Nativity
of Saint John the Baptist and to continue through all
that day And the third Fair or Mart of the said four
Fairs or Marts commencing on the day of Saint Bartholomew and also to continue through all that day And
the fourth Fair or Mart of the said four Fairs or Marts
commencing on the day of the Feast of Saint Simion
and Jude and to continue during all that day together
with a Court of Piedpoudre to be holden there at the
time of the said Fairs or Marts and together with all
liberties and free customs to such Courts pertaining
together with Stallage piccage fines and amerciaments
and all other profits commodities and emoluments
whatsoever to such Markets Fairs and Marts and to

the aforesaid Court of Piedpoudre pertaining happening arising or renewing and with all other free customs and liberties to such Fairs or Marts and Court of Piedpoudre pertaining or belonging REN-DERING yearly to us our Heirs and Successors out of and for the aforesaid fines amerciaments profits commodities and emoluments to the aforesaid Marts or Fairs and Courts of Piedpoudre pertaining or belonging the annual rent or farm of Three pounds by the year at the receipt of our Exchequer at Westminster payable at the Feast of Saint Michael the Archangel yearly AND WE WILL and by these presents for us our Heirs and Successors DO GRANT to the aforesaid Mayor Aldermen and Burgesses of the borough of Newbery aforesaid and to their Successors that the Mayor of the borough aforesaid for the time being shall have the survey and correction of all Victuals bought or sold or hereafter to be bought or sold in the borough aforesaid And also the examination correction and amendment of all and all manner of weights and measures within the borough of Newbery aforesaid MORE-OVER WE HAVE GRANTED and for us our Heirs and Successors WE DO GRANT to the aforesaid Mayor Aldermen and Burgesses of the borough aforesaid and to their Successors that the Mayor Steward and one of the Aldermen of the same borough by the Mayor and major part of the Capital Burgesses of the borough aforesaid for the time being from time to time to be elected during the time when they shall happen to be in such Offices shall be Justices and every of them shall be a Justice of us and of our Heirs and Successors as well to keep the Peace in the same Borough and the Liberties and Precincts of the same as to execute the Statutes concerning Vagabonds Artificers and Labourers and of weights and measures to be kept and corrected within the borough aforesaid and the Liberties and Precincts thereof AND that the same Mayor Steward and one of the Aldermen of the same Borough so as aforesaid to be chosen or any two of them (of whom the Mayor of the borough aforesaid for the time being We will to be one) shall execute and do all other things which to the office of Justice of the Peace pertain or belong in manner as any Keepers or Justices of the Peace in any County of our Realm of England ought or can have power to do by the Laws and Statutes of the same Kingdom of England AND WE WILL and by these presents DO GRANT for us our Heirs and Successors to the aforesaid Mayor Aldermen and Burgesses of the borough aforesaid and their Successors for ever that the same Mayor Steward and Aldermen and their Successors for the time being or any two of them (of whom the Mayor for the time being We will to be one) may and shall have power for ever to enquire hear conclude and determine all and singular trespasses offences defaults things matters and articles which to the Office of Justice of the Peace within the borough aforesaid the Liberties and Precincts thereof pertain to be done as fully and entirely and in as ample manner and form as any other Justices of our Peace and those of our Heirs and Successors in any County within our Kingdom of England may or shall be able to enquire hear or determine by the laws and statutes of our said Kingdom of England NEVER-THELESS so that the aforesaid Mayor Steward and Aldermen of the same borough for the time being or their Successors hereafter in nowise proceed to the determination of any murder or felony or any other matter touching the loss of life or limb within the borough aforesaid or the Liberties or Precincts of the same without the special mandate of us our Heirs or Successors AND WE WILL and by these presents for us our Heirs and Successors do grant to the aforesaid Mayor Aldermen and Burgesses of the borough aforesaid and their Successors that the Mayor Aldermen and Burgesses of the borough aforesaid and their Successors hereafter for ever may have hold use and enjoy and may and shall be able fully to have hold use and enjoy for ever all the same and the like lawful gifts grants liberties markets profits courts leet views of frankpledge lawdays exemptions privileges franchises acquittances articles and customs which the Burgesses of the borough aforesaid or which the Inhabitants of the same borough by whatsoever name or names of incorporation or by force of any incorporation by any Charter Letters Patents or Grants of us or of any one of the Progenitors or by any lawful custom or prescription heretofore lawfully had held or enjoyed AND all and singular the same for us our Heirs and Successors as much as in us lieth to the aforesaid Mayor Aldermen and Burgesses of the borough aforesaid and to their Successors for ever of our especial grace WE do by tenor of these presents approve and confirm by these presents in manner as our present Charter and these our Letters aforesaid reasonably testify WHEREFORE WE WILL and do firmly command for us our Heirs and Successors that the aforesaid Mayor Aldermen and Burgesses of the borough aforesaid and their Successors may have hold use and enjoy and may and shall be able for ever freely to have use and enjoy all liberties authorities and acquittances and other the premises aforesaid according to the tenor and effect of these our Letters Patent without the hindrance or impediment of us our Heirs or Successors our Justices Sheriffs or other Bailiffs or Ministers of us our Heirs and Successors whomsoever ALSO WE WILL and by these presents

DO GRANT to the aforesaid Mayor Aldermen and Burgesses of the borough aforesaid that they may and shall have these our Letters Patent under our Great Seal of England in due manner made and sealed without fine or fee great or small to us in our hanaper or elsewhere to our use to be therefore in anywise rendered paid or made **ALTHOUGH** express mention &c. **IN WITNESS** whereof &c. **WITNESS** the **QUEEN** at Westminster the 28th day of May

By Writ of Privy Seal,

A true Translation

W. ILLINGWORTH.

FINIS.

M. P. Price, Printer, Newbury.

PRINTED AND SOLD BY

M. P. PRICE,

MARKETPLACE, NEWBURY.

—»»◎◉◎««—

WHERE ALSO MAY BE HAD,

The History of

JACK OF NEWBURY.

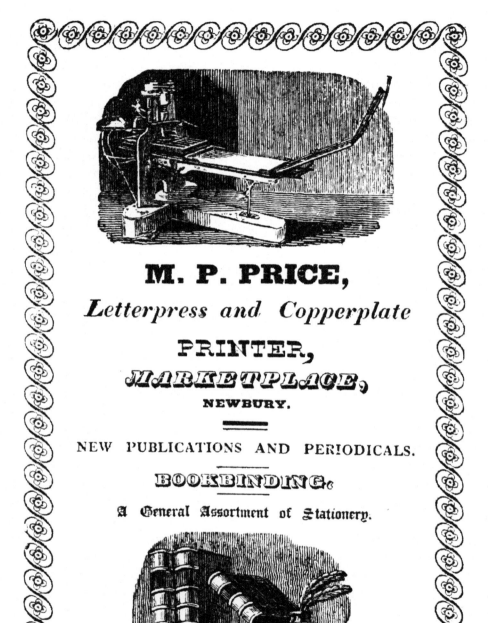

M. P. PRICE,

Letterpress and Copperplate

PRINTER,

MARKETPLACE,

NEWBURY.

===

NEW PUBLICATIONS AND PERIODICALS.

===

BOOKBINDING.

A General Assortment of Stationery.

CPSIA information can be obtained
at www.ICGtesting.com
Printed in the USA
BVOW07s2035180917

495170BV00012B/337/P